BOOK ONE

PLUTO AS A NATAL PLANET

The Plutonian Experience; The Discovery of Pluto; Pluto, Ruler Of Scorpio; Pluto In Cancer Through The Houses; Pluto In Leo Through The Houses; Pluto In Virgo Through The Houses; Pluto In Libra Through The Houses; Pluto In Scorpio Through The Houses; Natal Pluto In Aspect To Natal Planets.

BOOK TWO

PLUTO IN TRANSIT

Transiting Planets To Natal Pluto; Transiting Pluto To Natal Placements.

BOOK THREE

PLUTO AND THE FUTURE

Transiting Pluto Inside The Orbit Of Neptune; Major Transits To Pluto: 1978-2000; Conclusion.

The COMPLETE BOOK on

The POWER of PLUTO

The COMPLETE BOOK on The POWER of PLUTO

by
ARLENE ROBERTSON
and
MARGARET WILSON

The authors wish to express their appreciation to astrologers Lois Rodden, Joan McEvers, and Marc Penfield for generously sharing many of the birth times used in this book.

P.O. Box 1074
Birmingham, Michigan 48012

Cover Art Work: "The Power of Pali" by Pat Brown, San Francisco, California; depicts the Hawaiian goddess who resides in the volcanos of the islands, and watches over her people at all times.

ISBN 0-930-706-02-1

CONTENTS

BOOK ONE
PLUTO AS A NATAL PLANET

BOOK THREE
PLUTO AND THE FUTURE

In my end is my beginning.

T. S. Eliot

BOOK ONE

PLUTO AS A NATAL PLANET

INTRODUCTION
THE PLUTONIAN EXPERIENCE

For each one of us, sooner or later, the Plutonian experience erupts from the depths of our souls.

It comes upon us at different times, in the dark hours of the night, in the clear sunshine of day, in the fading twilight of the afternoon. Life batters and bruises us in many ways, and through it all, a basic pattern, a universality of experience, emerges. There are just so many things that can happen to us in this existence. We lose a beloved through death. We are rejected and abandoned by someone we love. We stand mute and helpless while a hard-won career shatters to pieces around us. We are stricken with a dread disease which extracts its terrible toll. Through it all, we have wrestled with grief and rage, the disillusionments, the agonies, the betrayals. We have all cried in the night. We have all made the journey into the depths of our being. We have—all of us—been there.

And so it comes upon us, this Plutonian experience. We realize the moment of decision is now. There is no one to help. There is no place to hide.

The way out is to go within. Irrevocably, the starting point is up to each one of us, as we stand alone and unafraid, at the crossroads of Destiny.

We make our choice, and having made it, a feeling of peace and serenity comes upon us. The fears of the future fade; faith in ourself returns as we release the old self-defeating ways and joyfully open our hearts and minds to the new beginning.

This is rebirth. This is renewal. *This* is the Plutonian Experience, and Pluto is the gut level of the soul.

THE DISCOVERY OF PLUTO

On January 21, 1930, the planet Pluto was discovered by Clyde Tombaugh of the Lowell Observatory in Flagstaff, Arizona. An extensive search had begun years before by Percival Lowell, an astronomer, who predicted from the perturbations in the orbits of Neptune and Uranus, the possibilities of another planet in our solar system. He did not live to see his prophecy come true.

Astronomers and mathematicians have determined that Pluto is 3,666,000,000 miles from the sun. The distance is so great that its astronomical body can barely be seen, even with the most powerful telescope; for this reason, its diameter cannot be accurately measured. It takes approximately 248.43 years for the planet to make a complete revolution around the Sun. It follows an eccentric orbit, which, in 1978, takes it inside the orbit of Neptune for twenty years, thus bringing it closer to the earth. It has been calculated from the variations of light reflected from Pluto, that it rotates on its axis in 6.4 days, which is slower than the rotations of Uranus and Neptune.

The astrological world selected the name Pluto, meaning lord of the underworld, from Greek mythology. Its most commonly used glyph, ♇ combines both the initials of its discoverer, Percival Lowell, and the first two letters of its name.

On the day of its discovery, Pluto was positioned at 18 degrees, 18 minutes of Cancer, opposing Mars at 18 degrees Capricorn. The Sun was positioned at 0 degrees Aquarius and Mercury, retrograde, at 1 degree, 56 minutes of Aquarius.

PLUTO THE RULER OF SCORPIO

The two-fold symbolism of Scorpio is described as the eagle soaring in the sky, strong and free, and the serpent lurking in dark corners, ready to strike and spread its poison. A third quality is suggested by the legend of the Phoenix bird which consumed itself by fire and, from its ashes, rose again.

These three symbols find their rightful place in the influences of the planet Pluto: power and control, domination and destruction, and renewal from a death-like experience. Thus the sign of Scorpio and the planet Pluto are tightly interwoven in their manifestation. It is now generally accepted among astrologers, after years of such observations, that Pluto rules Scorpio, releasing Mars to become the exclusive province of Aries.

Pluto is, therefore, power: Scorpio power. In the birth-chart, it intensifies the force of the sign it inhabits, its energies, attitudes, motivations, as well as its deficiencies. Since it remains in each sign for approximately twenty years, and in the case of Cancer, for twenty-five years, it creates a generational influence which can be likened to the backdrop on the stage setting against which the life stories of the characters are played. All the people born with Pluto in Cancer have a different basic approach to living than those, for example, with Pluto in Leo.

Since Pluto was discovered in 1930, while in the sign of Cancer, this treatise will cover its disposition in the signs it has traversed in our lifetimes: Cancer, Leo, Virgo, Libra and Scorpio.

When Pluto was discovered, we, as human beings, were ready to search our inner feelings, to contemplate the soul dwelling therein and to grapple for the understanding of our individualization. Never before in the recorded history of the world had such soul-searching occupied the masses. In centuries past only highly educated individuals had the time or the desire to probe into the darkness of the psyche and to fathom their patterns of behavior. People were preoccupied with earning a living, in battling the elements and in keeping the family clothed and fed. Deep philosophies and analytical discussions were beyond the range of thought. Religion was a refuge in time of trouble and from these beliefs one drew forth the strength to persevere from one day to the next.

Now that civilization provides the necessities of daily living with comparative ease, people have begun asking themselves, "Why am I this way? How can I best function in this world? How can I achieve a better life?" The opiate of blind obedience to religious concepts no longer suffices as the tension and turbulence of the twentieth century settle down on the brow of humanity.

Thus, the discovery of Pluto, the evolving planet, took place. Pluto's influence is subtle, traveling billions of miles through the cosmos before its vibrations reach us on earth. We who are living today, are the first mass of human beings to grow up under the forces generated by this mighty planet. We are indeed different from those who have gone before. The eternal challenge to live in peace and harmony with our fellow beings is battered on all sides by the widespread sins of our self-made world.

Pluto has been called the planet of the twentieth century. It can show us the way out of our twentieth century madness if we can embrace its inspirational message to 'Know Thyself,' to discard the refuse in the soul, to cleanse the heart and mind, and to follow the Light of guidance towards a new and better tomorrow.

CHAPTER ONE
PLUTO IN CANCER

TO PLUTO IN CANCER
INVICTUS

Out of the night that covers me,
Black as the Pit from pole to pole,
I thank whatever gods may be
For my unconquerable soul.

In the fell clutch of circumstance
I have not winced nor cried aloud,
Under the bludgeonings of chance
My head is bloody but unbowed.

Beyond this place of wrath and tears
Looms but the horror of the shade,
And yet the menace of the years
Finds, and shall find me, unafraid.

It matters not how strait the gate,
How charged with punishments the scroll,
I am the master of my fate;
I am the captain of my soul.

—William Ernest Henley

PLUTO IN CANCER
THE GENERATIONAL INFLUENCES

September 24, 1912 to October 2, 1912; July 12, 1913 to December 25, 1913; May 23, 1914 to October 8, 1937; November 15, 1937 to August 5, 1938; February 7, 1939 to June 15, 1939.

Millions of people living today have the planet Pluto in Cancer in their birth charts. Cancer signifies home and family and is the natural ruler of the fourth house from which our roots grow. It is here we gather our strength and substance, where we are molded and formed to project ourselves into a hostile world.

This, then, is the hearthstone generation that grew to maturity surrounded by the security of the home. Our mothers fulfilled the accepted behavioral role of the times, nurturing and protecting us in a strong emotional bond. She greeted us lovingly after school, listened patiently to our stories of daily happenings and dutifully encouraged us to make good grades and study our music lessons. She kept us well-fed and properly clothed. In manners and deportment, she was the supreme authority, instructing us frequently on thoughtful consideration of others and their possessions. We were told to be courteous to the neighbors and to show deference to the elderly. In return for her loving warmth, she looked for and usually received, obedience and respect for her position.

To oppose mother's rules was to invite rejection and disaster.

Father, as he was called then, brought a sense of domination and control to the family circle. He was often an awesome figure with his mysterious ability to make money and supply us with the necessities of existence which we humbly accepted. He constantly stressed to us all the rewards of hard work, honesty and dependability. The value of an education was close to his heart and he impressed upon us the vast opportunities available to anyone with the ambition to pursue them. He yearned to raise his children a little higher up the ladder than he had been able to go. If he were an educated man in one of the professions, he naturally expected that his sons would follow in his footsteps. His daughters, he assumed, would behave like ladies, be grateful for their education and, in due time, enter into a respectable marriage with fine, healthy children arriving at the proper intervals. It was imperative that the family name be carried on.

Our pleasures were simple ones, sharing a peanut butter sandwich and a glass of milk with our best friend, turning cartwheels on the grass, reading to each other from our favorite books, playing hop-scotch or jumping rope, riding our bicycles down to the corner grocery store on errands. On Sundays, we piled into the family car and drove out to the countryside or picnicked at a public park. A day-long trip to the mountains or the seashore was a rare and exciting event. We matured in an era untouched by war, television, drugs, pornography, polluted water and air, the birth control pill, take-home dinners and frozen pizza.

Grandparents, uncles and aunts played an integral part in our daily lives, passing along a concept of dignity in our heritage and an understanding of our roots. Often several generations lived, more or less amicably, under the same roof of the big, sturdy three-story homes. Mingling together, enjoying and learning from each other, we grew up with a strong family pride, a bulwark against the terrors of the outside world. We toed the mark and obeyed the rules. Those were the days when we knew what the rules were.

Divorce occurred rarely, mostly among movie stars and glamorous society figures. If the participants were from the middle or lower economic classes, they were not readily accepted into the social sphere, but rather were looked upon with suspicion and mistrust and were often shunned.

The depression years made indelible marks upon us all. We can remember when families, friends, and neighbors strove to put food on the table, pay the rent or the mortgage, find an honest day's work for a dollar or two. We saved the two-cent newspaper and passed it along, ate a lot of potatoes at a penny a pound, and wore our faded and handed-down clothes uncomplainingly. Along the way we learned to survive on the barest necessities and the strength we gained then is still deeply ingrained in us all.

This, then, is the generation that experienced

from the security of the family circle the drastic upheavals of the times; prohibition, the rise of gangsterism, economic collapse, widespread unemployment and the startling changes of the early Roosevelt years. This is the generation that came of age and answered the rallying call to protect and defend our country against the common enemy in the hour of our greatest need. Millions of young men, born between 1912 and 1927 became the G. I. Joes of World War II. Millions of women laid down their paring knives and mixing spoons, picked up the riveting guns and the welding torches and hurried off to work in the factories and shipyards, turning out the supplies urgently needed in an accelerated war. All of these people had Pluto in Cancer, and never before, or since, has this nation felt the strong sense of unity and the common bond of its citizenry as it was freely expressed then.

Our deeply felt patriotism is one of the strongest forces of Pluto in Cancer people. In our youth we gave the Pledge of Allegiance every day in school, knew all the words to "America, the Beautiful" and saluted our flag with pride. Scratch a man or woman anywhere over forty and you will find the beating heart of a patriot. We all feel deeply, that in spite of its faults, its overwhelming problems and its occasional monumental mistakes, this is still the greatest country in the world.

We are still around in large numbers, we Pluto in Cancer people, somewhat battered and bruised, looking about in bewilderment, struggling to adjust to the constantly shifting and changing moral codes and standards of the world today. Many of us look back longingly, in Cancer fashion, to the years when we understood what the rules were and how we tallied up the score. We have experienced total metamorphosis. The world we live in now is no longer the world we knew when we were young.

This is the power of Pluto in Cancer, to mark a generation deeply with the intrinsic and unshakeable values of country, family and home.

PLUTO IN CANCER THROUGH THE HOUSES

In the study of astrology, the difficulty arises in presenting a single planetary placement by itself with no indication of its inter-relationship to the other nine planets. This is, of course, almost impossible to cover in a textbook due to the innumerable conditions which must be considered in any delineation.

In an effort to assist the reader in applying the Pluto interpretations as presented in this book, the following list will delineate the level of importance that Pluto in Cancer may assume when found in the following situations:

1. Pluto is most powerful when the natal Sun is

in Scorpio or when there is a stellium (three or more planets), in Scorpio.

2. Pluto is powerful when it is in Cancer's natural fourth house, or in its own natural eighth house.

3. The power of Pluto is intensified if it is conjunct the Moon, in Cancer.

4. If Pluto is square the Moon in Aries or Libra, the emotional difficulties will be felt strongly through personal relationships.

5. If Pluto opposes the Moon in Capricorn, the two opposites are set into motion, releasing forces which are in conflict and need to be resolved. The area for growth is represented by the house position of the Moon.

6. If Pluto is trine the Moon in Pisces, the emotions flow freely into normal healthy outlets. If Pluto is trine the Moon in Scorpio, a mutual reception exists and the energies of the two planets will strengthen each other in a positive way.

7. If Pluto is sextile the Moon in Taurus, or Virgo, an opportunity for growth is present in the houses governed by these signs.

8. If Pluto is quincunx the Moon in Sagittarius, or Aquarius, tension and strain result because the two planets are not in the same element, and are uncomfortable with each other. One may often find that a health aspect is involved.

9. If Pluto is semisextile the Moon in Gemini, or Leo, no special interplay occurs. It is a neutral aspect.

PLUTO IN CANCER IN THE FIRST HOUSE

These natives are often viewed as outstanding individuals projecting an air of strength and a subtle aura of mystery. They perceive life and its experiences directly through their senses, for their daily existence flows endlessly in a river of emotional reactions to their surroundings, and to those persons in their environment.

The female in this case becomes mother in the conventional sense of the word, by caring for her children and husband with deep devotion and willingly sacrificing herself to their pleasures and demands. The male will deal with the situation on a larger basis from his place in the community. Whatever his position, in the professional, medical or business field, he will look upon the people involved in his sphere of activity as his family.

Here the individuals' search for power may manifest in masterful control of self. Such discipline will carry them through the inevitable tragedies and upheavals of a lifetime. When they face defeat, when the world falls into a shambles, they will dredge up from the depths the dynamic energy of Pluto, to revitalize and steer them through.

Negatively they can turn this inner-strength into artful and deceptively strong maneuvering of others. Their method involves bewildering their opponents and plastering them with guilt. To win out they may passively withdraw from the battlefield leaving behind frustrated and bewildered adversaries who, finding weapons useless, succumb to the natives' demands.

With this placement, Scorpio falls in the fifth house of self-expression and creativity, generating intense emotional forces. These natives have a vital need to find productive and satisfying outlets for their interests. Whatever they enjoy—physical activity in sports, acting in theatre groups, growing the best tomatoes—they should pursue ardently and allow their abilities to blossom. If they think they have no talents, and that it is all rather unimportant, the blockage may bring on illness caused by frustrating the urgent need for expression.

At first meeting, these individuals often arouse feelings of uneasiness in others because of their quiet intensity. Underneath the veneer of assurance they may suffer from a sense of inferiority. To compensate, they constantly reach for the Cancerian security of the home with the family gathered around in a closely knit group. Only then can they be sure of themselves. Being so emotionally sensitive they seldom lash out in times of crisis, because they fear that others too may unleash their negative feelings, and always they act to protect themselves against pain.

Physically, the native will likely have a round face, with soft features, heavy-lidded eyes and short stubby fingers will small fingernails. The women will be pleasantly curvy in contour. If the Moon is placed in another element—air, fire or earth—the appearance will be modified accordingly.

PEOPLE BORN WITH PLUTO IN CANCER IN THE FIRST HOUSE

1. Robert McNamara, former Secretary of Defense:[6] June 9, 1916, 5:45 a.m. PST, San Francisco, California.
2. Dinah Shore, TV hostess and singer:[6] February 29, 1916, 11:45 a.m. CST, Winchester, Tennessee.
3. Henry Kissinger, former Secretary of State:[3] May 27, 1923, 5:30 a.m. ST, Furth, Germany.
4. Merv Griffin, TV host and singer:[1] July 6, 1925, 4:45 a.m. PST, San Mateo, California.
5. David Frost, TV host and writer:[3] April 7, 1939, 10:29 a.m. GMT, Tenterden, Kent, England.

PLUTO IN CANCER IN THE SECOND HOUSE

In Venus' natural house, the natives' values are involved with the need to be nurtured and loved for themselves. All their life they seek the fulfillment of a deeply felt yearning for a close relationship and a strong family unit. They may never find it if, along the way, the search for worldly success becomes more important. Ultimately they may realize that money cannot buy that which they desire so intensely.

"What are my values?" they may ask. "How do I feel about myself? What has made me happy?" In whatever house it inhabits, Pluto demands that the native find the right perspective in that area of life. The regeneration may take twenty to twenty-five years while Pluto is transiting the sign. These people may be totally unaware of the change occurring, until they look back and, from a long range view, recognize that their values have been transformed. Their emotional fulfillment will then be wrapped up in love and not in the pursuit of money. They have learned that their security lies within the self and in so doing, will discover their finer qualities and their own self-worth. Only then can they allow their feelings, complete in their full natural scope, to be unlocked, freeing any conflicts from deep within their being.

In the workaday world they will labor industriously to provide the family with the necessities of existence and, having achieved this, will put their efforts into supplying them with the luxurious comforts of our present day life style—the television sets, the barbecue pit and the swimming pool. At the end of a long hard day, after manipulating money in the establishment, they look forward to relaxing in an easy chair in the cozy recreation room with the family gathered around.

The Cancer tendencies are often shown in the market place by anticipating the newest trends in manufacturing, merchandising and selling. What will the public buy for the old homestead, the ranch house or the condominium? With Pluto placed here, the native instinctively knows, and many have made millions climbing on the bandwagon ahead of the crowd. They have, however, no inclination to gamble with the family security. The nest egg stays in the bank.

Scorpio's natural eighth house opposes this placement. Thus, the native can often sense, in Cancerian fashion, hidden possibilities in a business deal, or ferret out secret information involving others which may prove to be an invaluable guide toward financial success. They have the talent to turn liabilities into assets. However, with Saturnian Capricorn on the eighth house cusp they will probably experience frustration in any efforts to involve themselves with partners and ultimately will be more successful striking out on their own.

Negatively, the Pluto power can wield money as a weapon of control by using bribes and other dishonest methods to achieve self-centered goals.

PEOPLE BORN WITH PLUTO IN CANCER IN THE SECOND HOUSE

1. Gerald R. Ford, former U.S. President:[5] July 14, 1913, 12:43 a.m. CST, Omaha, Nebraska.
2. Gregory Peck, actor:[7] April 5, 1916, 8:00 a.m., La Jolla, California.
3. Phyllis Diller, comedienne:[5] July 17, 1917, 1:00 a.m. CST, Lima, Ohio.
4. Rod Serling, author:[6] December 25, 1924, 3:15 p.m. EST, Syracuse, New York.
5. Harry Belafonte, singer and actor:[5] March 1, 1927, 10:30 a.m. EST, New York, New York.

PLUTO IN CANCER IN THE THIRD HOUSE

With the combination of Plutonian power and Mercurial influence, this placement produces the forceful, penetrating speaker who holds the audience spellbound. Aided by Cancerian intuition and a remarkable vocabulary, these natives approach their listeners at the latter's own level of understanding. They deliver their message with enthusiasm, diplomacy and tact. Here, also, turbulent emotions are computerized and filtered through the airy stimulation of Gemini. They say to themselves, "I think I feel deeply about this."

If they use these talents negatively they can become people who demand constant attention, monopolize conversations, trap friends into listening to long-winded monologues and inflict ideas and experiences relentlessly on everyone. The speech may be peppered with vulgar phrases tossed in for shock effect. Here, the native must learn to use the powers of communication in a constructive manner.

With Scorpio on the seventh house cusp, a strong urge for a partner will be felt. They will be attracted to someone with Scorpio qualities and, for a successful relationship, should seek out one who has the same level of understanding, one who operates on the same intellectual level.

The native will probe into many areas in search for knowledge, especially the study of history and their own family lineage. In work, they may be involved with secret information or travel frequently on strange missions. They will delight in solving mysteries which confound others. This talent could be channeled into writing detective stories as well as science fiction, a creative outlet for these energies.

This is the family member who will speak out for their brothers and sisters and, if the eldest, may take on the role of mothering them, listening to their troubles and playing amateur counselor. This association with siblings may continue throughout life. In a neighborhood where many children play together their impulses may lead them to mothering the whole flock. They are natural baby-sitters.

Neighbors come into this range also. The natives' curiosity and strong urge to communicate may involve them in neighborhood activities, such as helping others with gardening, house repairs, sampling their cooking or borrowing books. Such experiences during youth may lead them into marriage with a neighbor or childhood sweetheart.

PEOPLE BORN WITH PLUTO IN CANCER IN THE THIRD HOUSE

1. Robert F. Kennedy, former Attorney General:[3] November 20, 1925, 3:10 p.m. EST, Brookline, Massachusetts.
2. Martin Luther King, Jr., religious leader, civil rights activist:[8] January 15, 1929, 11:20 a.m. CST, Atlanta, Georgia.

3. Burt Reynolds, actor:[1] February 11, 1936, 12:10 p.m. EST, Lansing, Michigan.
4. Tom Snyder, TV talk show host:[3] May 12, 1936, 5:30 a.m. CST, Milwaukee, Wisconsin.
5. Neil Armstrong, astronaut, first man on the moon:[3] August 5, 1939, 00:30 a.m. EST, Wapakoneta, Ohio.

PLUTO IN CANCER IN THE FOURTH HOUSE

The sign of Cancer in its own natural house is a powerful placement. Our roots grow from the depths of the fourth house and with Pluto's presence here, they are indeed strong ones. Here, also, the water triplicity ripples forth from its natural houses, with Scorpio on the eight and Pisces on the twelfth, making a trine to Cancer. A copious flow of emotions and psychic sensitivity washes over these natives in all areas of life. They must learn to control their feelings, and use them to their advantage, or otherwise too much emotional display can turn them into a quivering mass of nervous reaction.

One of the strongest roots is entwined around the natives' unhappy memories of childhood, which are still as vivid and dramatic as the moment when first lived. They are often so preoccupied with such remembrances that they are distracted in their daily routine. Tenacious Cancer must learn to let go of such depressing thoughts, cleaning out the closet of the mind when it becomes dangerously cluttered. They should strive to replace these negative patterns with new and happy experiences.

In their own home, where the roots run deep, these natives expect to be lord and master with their authority discreetly recognized. If this does not occur with ease, an insidious, endless power-struggle involving all of the family may take place over the years.

The loss of the father may result in a deep emotional attachment to the mother and, if formed in early childhood, may color the entire life. Should this transpire, the person may experience great difficulty with motivation, especially when relating to women. In the case of a male, he may never marry, or he may suffer many unhappy relationships. In the case of a female, the absence of a father may cause her to search throughout her life for a worthy substitute to fulfill her emotional needs.

If the mother dies, the person may constantly seek one who can give the nurturing care that was lacking during childhood.

These natives will harbor the magnificent obsession to make a home of their own, complete, inviolate, secure. They will yearn to possess not only the land the house is built upon, but also other acreage to provide insurance against the trauma of deprivation.

Responding to another negative influence, the natives may turn against their ethnic or religious heritage by severing all family ties, changing their name and moving a long distance away.

Career possibilities may incline the individual towards all forms of real estate and construction, mining and underground enterprises. The Moon rules silver, and Pluto, uranium, so a natural outlet could occur in the mining of these metals.

On the positive side, the atmosphere of the home will be one of refinement and tender loving care. Cancerians enjoy dispensing the hospitality of the household: wonderful, soul-satisfying food, delicious drinks, happy conversations, and for the frequent overnight guests, comfortable beds with sweet-smelling sheets and sparkling bathrooms with fluffy towels. Many Cancer people collect memorabilia which they proudly display to their friends. They are also known for their persistence in hanging on to possessions and seldom if ever, will they clean out bulging closets and crowded shelves.

PEOPLE BORN WITH PLUTO IN CANCER IN THE FOURTH HOUSE

1. Carol Burnett, TV comedienne:[3] April 26, 1933, 4:15 a.m. CST, San Antonio, Texas.
2. F. Lee Bailey, lawyer:[5] June 10, 1933, 2:00 a.m. EST, Waltham, Massachusetts.
3. Charles Manson, murderer:[3] November 12, 1934, 4:40 p.m. EST, Cincinnati, Ohio.
4. Elvis Presley, singer and actor:[9] January 8, 1935, 12:20 p.m. CST, East Tupelo, Mississippi.

5. Mary Tyler Moore, TV comedienne, actress:[2] December 29, 1937, 12:15 p.m. EST, Brooklyn, New York.

PLUTO IN CANCER IN THE FIFTH HOUSE

Here the natives' strongest motivation coalesces in the desire to love and be loved with passionate intensity. Love affairs will be marked with frenzy, eroticism and romantic fantasies, for these natives will see in the beloved what they wish to see, overlooking the mundane and dreary to wander down the byways of illusion and enchantment. Nor will each affair ever be totally finished. Always some part of the Cancer character will be obstinately holding on, leaving the door open and hoping that the lover will forgive, forget and come crawling back to begin anew another turbulent relationship. At some time in their lives, these individuals must perceive that their ability to love should hold a quality of generosity, given freely and unselfishly, with no strings attached. Then will they truly understand their tremendous emotional capacity.

These natives have a strong desire for children and feel empty and unfulfilled without them. The normal parental instincts can flow from them easily as they embrace the young ones in sheer delight at their good fortune. On the other hand, if they overdo the Cancerian possessiveness, they can stifle a child's individuality and turn it into a puppet on a string. If not blessed with offspring, they will be inclined to adopt them. The younger the child, the better; in this way, they can raise the child as their own.

The Pluto influence may manifest in the birth of only one child to the native, and that one possibly being born late in the parent's life.

With Scorpio on the ninth house cusp, much satisfaction will be derived from all forms of higher learning. Such education may be achieved in later life, particularly for the woman who raises her family first and then returns to the academic fold when they have grown. Men may also experience delays in their early years as a result of financial pressures, and in seeking to round out their knowledge, find pride in their achievements later on.

Since Leo's natural house encompasses social activities, these Pluto-in-Cancer natives take their parties seriously. The busy Cancer hostess who has worked for many hours in preparation for her succulent feast, needs to be told by her guests that her carrot cake is, indeed, delicious; while the hospitable host mixing the drinks wants his expert bartending to be appreciated.

PEOPLE BORN WITH PLUTO IN CANCER IN THE FIFTH HOUSE

1. Eugene McCarthy, former Senator:[6] March 29, 1916, 4:00 a.m. CST, Watkins, Minnesota.
2. Norman Mailer, author:[6] January 31, 1923, 9:05 a.m. EST, Long Branch, New Jersey.

3. Walter Mondale, Vice President of the U.S.:[6] January 5, 1928, 10:30 a.m. CST, Ceylon, Minnesota.
4. Ethel Kennedy, wife of Robert F. Kennedy:[5] April 11, 1928, 3:30 a.m. CST, Chicago, Illinois.
5. Robert Redford, actor:[13] August 18, 1936, 8:02 p.m. PST, Santa Monica, California.

PLUTO IN CANCER IN THE SIXTH HOUSE

A blending of cardinal and fixed in a mutable house suggests that these individuals would do well in occupations allowing them to initiate and consolidate activities in their work. They seek the opportunity to utilize their special skills in the labor market. Once this happens they will exert influence to improve conditions and may bring about many worthwhile changes. They may become aggressive in championing the rights of other fellow workers.

These individuals need the emotional outlet provided in service to others, which may be found in their job or in daily contacts with family and friends. If they work too hard trying to please everyone, the resulting stress may manifest in hypochondria or psychosomatic illness. They must learn to temper the desire to help with common sense and a long range view. A definite conflict may arise between work and health and the necessity of finding the key to put both in perspective.

In the field of medicine, their psychic abilities could be channeled into an understanding of their patients' feelings and actual physical sufferings. They can pick up the vibrations of others and in doing so, may fathom not only what the person needs, but also what is not needed. Such information could be invaluable. Their talents, which are reinforced with the Cancerian need to care for and nurture, may find expression in all functions of medicine and nursing.

Because of their active imaginations, these people should avoid any negative thoughts of possible illness, for needless worry and confusion would result. Their interest in holistic health will ripen and, in learning to care for their own body, they may be led into the study of nutrition and research on the dangers of food additives and preservatives. Once this curiosity is thoroughly aroused they may spread their knowledge of sensible health care to everyone, and along the way become some of the world's greatest healthful-living enthusiasts.

The Plutonian power may bend in another direction, towards a military career. This would also be an excellent choice, for this placement combines the ability to organize, the understanding of one's compatriots, a passion for doing one's duty and an abiding love of country.

The native can also find productive expression in dealing with governmental atomic energy plants or those businesses involved with salvaging and reclaiming materials for further use.

PEOPLE BORN WITH PLUTO IN CANCER IN THE SIXTH HOUSE

1. Jonas Salk, developer of the polio vaccine:[6] October 28, 1914, 11:15 a.m. EST, New York, New York.
2. Beverly Sills, opera singer:[10] May 25, 1929, midnight EDT, Brooklyn, New York.
3. Ralph Nader, consumer activist:[3] February 27, 1934, 4:30 a.m. EST, Winsted, Connecticut.
4. Bill Moyers, journalist:[6] June 5, 1934, 11:15 p.m. CST, Hugo, Oklahoma.
5. John Dean, former White House counsel:[5] October 14, 1938, 2:55 p.m. EST, Akron, Ohio.

PLUTO IN CANCER IN THE SEVENTH HOUSE

With Libra ruling the natural seventh house, Pluto-in-Cancer individuals believe deeply in close relationships and are extremely sensitive to such involvements. Capricorn falls on the ascendant with this placement; therefore, the influence of Saturn is felt in the native's need for a strong partner.

Here the man is searching for the ideal wife, one who stays home, raises the children, runs the house efficiently and shares his feelings about family ties. She enhances his status as a person of respectability and stature in the community.

His energies are focused on his position in the business world or into his profession and he expects her, as his partner, to function effectively in her capacity so that she mirrors his success. He is the one giving orders and she dutifully carries them out. Capricorn is independent; Cancer is dependent.

The Capricorn-rising woman may, in many cases, have lost a parent during her childhood years. Thus, the concept of a home as a place of security and a bastion against the hostile world represents a deeply ingrained need in her. She often searches for the father figure she may have lacked in her youth and, finding him in a husband, she is content to follow the traditions and allow him to rule. With Aries on the fourth house cusp she is endowed with considerable energy which she pours into her accepted role. If not properly handled the drive can be negatively used in the urge to dominate and manipulate her family. Her children's behavior, particularly in the public eye, and their achievements are extremely important to her and she enjoys shining in their reflected glory.

With the combination of Capricorn on the first and Aries on the fourth her compulsion to express her individuality would break out. This is not a woman who will sit in the back row all her life. She may discover that the most satisfying outlets lie in participating in community affairs and school happenings where her organizational ability would be put to good use. Since the Moon rules Cancer, the Pluto-in-Cancer placement, especially in the seventh house, is basically more comfortable and free-flowing in a woman's chart than in a man's.

As much as these natives want to be in control of their lives, they will get involved with others who will thwart them in a subtle manner. Tensions may develop in such situations. The position of Saturn in the chart will indicate how this can best be handled. Even if the individuals admire their seventh house partner, they will find it unbearable, at times, to relinquish control. They will want to establish authority over and over again, often in ways that might be considered questionable. Sooner or later, along life's pathway, they will be directed towards the regeneration of their close relationships by allowing others the freedom to express themselves as individuals.

Since seventh house contracts are binding, altered only by legal action, the natives take their marriage vows seriously. They are broken only after emotionally bruising experiences which leave an indelible mark. Usually the husband and wife find it impossible to remain friends and, if they allow their negative feelings to control them, they can turn into lifelong enemies. Each one wants his or her fair share of their worldly goods and often a stubborn, lengthy battle occurs in the courts. The wife will fight for her and her children's rightful portion of the property, which represents, once again, the Cancer inborn need for security. In the case of divorce, the Capricorn ascending man would worry considerably about his public image.

Scorpio is placed in the eleventh house stressing again the trine aspect of Pluto to its ruler. Significant and satisfying friendships, based both on the emotionality and loyalty of Cancer and Scorpio, would flourish. The native would be a true, caring, lifelong friend and relationships would represent quality, not quantity. In many cases, the native may discover the marriage partner in this circle of friends or in a group, club or association to which he or she belongs.

A business partner would be sought for the ability to sense what the public wants to buy. The native will be drawn to one who can supply financial backing and who will supervise their joint investments. With the Capricorn business authority and the Cancer money-watching ability, these two would make a successful business team. The Cancer person knows how to mingle with the public and seek its favor.

PEOPLE BORN WITH PLUTO IN CANCER IN THE SEVENTH HOUSE

1. Spiro Agnew, former Vice President of the U.S.:[6] November 9, 1918, 9:00 a.m. EST, Forest Hills, Maryland.
2. Betty Friedan, leader of Women's Liberation Movement:[2] February 4, 1921, 4:00 a.m. CST, Peoria, Illinois.
3. Edward Kennedy, Senator:[3] February 22, 1932, 3:58 a.m. EST, Dorchester, Massachusetts.

4. Alan Alda, actor:[6] January 28, 1936, 5:07 a.m. EST, New York, New York.
5. Jane Fonda, actress:[2] December 21, 1937, 7:00 a.m. EST, New York, New York.

PLUTO IN CANCER IN THE EIGHTH HOUSE

Pluto in its own house activates tremendous power. The Scorpio qualities of intensity, depth and fixity are heavily indicated, permeating the basic meanings of this house. The surge of energies pouring forth here guarantees that sometime, in their lives, these natives will be born again.

The importance of the sexual expression cannot be underestimated. With the Cancer influence, the native is inclined to feel that the sex act is primarily meant as the means of producing children to fulfill the parenting instinct. Secondly, sex is for pleasure and if the partner is not compatible, the native will resort to clandestine affairs and hedonistic outlets to consummate the strong physical drive ingrained in Scorpio.

Eighth house natives are extremely sensitive to the death experience, particularly in the loss of a loved one. They find it almost impossible to let go of thoughts, memories and physical possessions of the beloved and to accept the fact that the person is no longer part of their world. The tenacity of Cancer and the rigidity of Scorpio combine their forces to create an insurmountable wall that other individuals, waiting on the fringes of the native's life, find it almost impossible to scale.

In many cases, the study of the occult, the after-life and reincarnation become vital interests. They search, often secretly, for the basic meanings of life and death. In time, touched by compassion, they may be led to the healing arts and to institutional work with the handicapped.

Pluto here also may bring about a life-or-death experience for these natives in a serious illness, a devastating accident, a searing emotional disaster. Having survived the catastrophe, they feel that in the true spiritual sense, they have been born again.

The resources that two people have gained or lost in a business or marriage relationship are also shown by the eighth house. The first house partners with Sagittarius on the ascendent, and Capricorn on the second, would have a conservative attitude about money. They would appreciate value and spend wisely for the best they could afford. Here is the original comparison shopper. They will not be cheated, nor will they put on a display of possessions or live beyond their means. Because they earned it themselves they have a healthy respect for a dollar. Taurus on the sixth, and Virgo on the tenth, set up an earth trine in the money houses. The tendency is towards a materialistic view of life.

PEOPLE BORN WITH PLUTO IN CANCER IN THE EIGHTH HOUSE

1. Marlon Brando, actor:[6] April 3, 1924, 10:37 p.m. CST, Omaha, Nebraska.

2. Gore Vidal, author:[6] October 3, 1925, 11:00 a.m. EST, West Point, New York.
3. Shirley Temple Black, former child movie star, ambassador:[3] April 23, 1928, 9:00 p.m. PST, Santa Monica, California.
4. Jacqueline Kennedy Onassis, former First Lady:[3] July 28, 1929, 2:30 p.m. EDT, Southhampton, New York.
5. Werner Erhardt, founder of est:[6] September 5, 1935, 12 noon EST, Philadelphia, Pennsylvania.

PLUTO IN CANCER IN THE NINTH HOUSE

Transiting Pluto, which is currently in Libra, squaring natal Pluto in Cancer, is a powerful transit which happens only once in a person's lifetime. The effect is potent and irrevocable as it digs underneath the surface, dredging up waste and debris which must be eliminated to bring about Plutonian renewal. Depending upon which house it is transiting, Pluto indicates that something must die so that a greater force can be born.

With Pluto in Cancer in Jupiter's ninth house of moral values, Libra, the natural ruler of the seventh house of marriage, is on the cusp of the twelfth house of the unconscious. Uranus, transiting through Libra from October 1968, to September 1975, brought about sudden disruptive changes in seventh house matters. Now Pluto follows behind to make order out of the chaos.

The individuals with this placement in their natal charts have undergone tremendous alterations in their lives caused by this transit. With the ninth house affected they have experienced in many cases a jolting change in their religious ideas, moral values, concept of marriage and the function of wife and mother in family life. Everything has come up for drastic review.

Concerning religion, many have questioned their lifelong acceptance of the doctrines instilled in childhood. The credos of the parents, learned so long ago, no longer offered substance and solace in a world spinning rapidly toward self-destruction. Old fashioned ideas were discarded, and the newer influences of the twentieth century were introduced. The metaphysical world came upon us through the sciences of the mind, awareness techniques and the eastern philosophies. An open, informal approach to one's basic beliefs was a refreshing change from the formalized structures of the past.

With the Libran influence, the institution of marriage, strictly controlled through the centuries, went through startling changes. For years women, trapped by the sexual mores and financial conditions of the times, had no other recourse but to submit meekly to playing secondary roles as wives and mothers. Now, suddenly, with the women's liberation movement gaining momentum, they have sought, and in many cases won, the right of equal pay for equal work and the opportunity to advance into positions hitherto classified as the exclusive province of the male.

Divorcees, single women and widows experimented with the now socially acceptable condition of living with a man without a marriage contract. They discovered a certain intriguing sense of adventure in sexual freedom. Moving in was simple; moving out was considerably easier than going through a messy, prolonged and often financially disastrous divorce. They delighted in their independence. Even though they had become involved in a close relationship, no longer were they going to play servant, picking up the dirty clothes, serving the cold glass of beer, dishing up the meat and potatoes promptly at six. If they eventually found the arrangement stifling and self-defeating, they could simply pack up their belongings and leave.

These women became their own persons, free to express their talents and pursue their interests which may have been overlooked or stifled for years. Many returned to colleges and universities to continue their education which had been interrupted by marriage and children. Others, left with a home too large for their needs, sold it, collected their possessions and hit the trail to another part of the country to start new lives unmarred by disturbing surroundings and negative influences. Many polished their neglected skills and found rewarding employment and financial independence.

It was not easy, however, for these Pluto-in-

Cancer women to shake loose from the old moral values instilled in them since childhood. With the blush of youth gone, they struggled to overcome the strictness of years of conforming to the rules. Their sense of security was threatened. No longer were they Mrs. Somebody, a role they had played for so long. Now they were just plain Jane Smith, trying to make it on their own. Many succeeded in achieving a rebirth in their lives while others are still striving to conquer the uneasiness plaguing them as they appear on the surface to accept the new morality. Cancer does not let go of the old ways easily.

During this period, many marriages of long duration—thirty years or more—fell apart and ended in the divorce court. Friends and acquaintances often were shocked when this happened. "It seemed like such a good marriage," they said. What had happened? To outsiders, the unhappy condition of the relationship was well-hidden because the principals for years had built a facade to fool the world. Both had held on from habit, unable to release this insidious form of negative emotional security. They had always told themselves, and each other, that it was best for the children and the husband's career to stay together. Later on, perhaps, when they had fulfilled their duties as parents they might discuss it and reach some amicable conclusion. Transiting Pluto, squaring natal Pluto, dredged it up from the inner depths and a decision had to be made. The marriage ended up as just another statistic in the records.

But the persons are still functioning as distinct individuals who have discarded that which is no longer of any value or substance, and are reaching out for a better life and a new beginning. Truly, this is the spirit of Phoenix rising up from the ashes of defeat to build again.

PEOPLE BORN WITH PLUTO IN CANCER IN THE NINTH HOUSE

1. John F. Kennedy, former President of the U.S.:[3] May 29, 1917, 3:00 p.m. EST, Brookline, Massachusetts.
2. Billy Graham, religious leader:[6] November 17, 1918, 4:28 a.m. EST, Charlotte, North Carolina.
3. Jimmy Carter, President of the U.S.:[5] October 1, 1924, 7:00 a.m. CST, Plains, Georgia.
4. Fidel Castro, Cuban Communist Premier:[6] August 13, 1926, 11:00 a.m. EST, Mayari, Oriente, Cuba.
5. Gloria Steinem, editor, writer, leader of Women's Liberation Movement:[2] March 25, 1934, 10:00 p.m. EST, Toledo, Ohio.

PLUTO IN CANCER IN THE TENTH HOUSE

The combination of Pluto in the tenth house of career, and Scorpio on the second house of money and values, produces individuals with an innate desire to achieve in the world. Instinctively, they know what the masses want and what they will buy in the market place. The drive for power is not only for personal recognition, but also to accumulate money, for they are well aware of the fact that money is power. Establishing values early in life they become a law unto themselves. However, the Cancer influence, representing the authority of the home and the nation, is felt in their adherence to the rules of the game. Unless they are bombarded with strong negative forces, they will be faithful to the Scorpio code of honesty and integrity.

Because of the Capricorn fourth house cusp, they may have been shunted into a corner in early years. As they mature and the compulsion to succeed gains momentum, they are saying, "Look at me, world. Nobody did when I was a child. I want to show you that I can make it on my own." With the fourth house representing a parent, they may have been manipulated and pushed into a career to satisfy some unrequited need of the parent. Here is the prototype of the stage mother who subtly directs the native to fulfill her vicarious desires to suceed in show business. Or it may be the father who names his son after himself to reflect his ego, and then expects the son to mirror his image.

With Libra on the ascendent these natives will be endowed with considerable charm and grace which will be valuable in their climb to the top. They will project these attributes easily.

The combination of Pluto-Cancer-Scorpio emotionally will dominate their ambitions so that their reactions are primarily sensory ones. The Scorpio fixity, in this case, exercises some control over what could be an overwhelming excess of feelings.

Plagued by memories of the past they may consider themselves failures even though in the eyes of the world they are a smashing success. They may become so obsessed with work that they devote all their waking hours to it, while the family and home life suffer from neglect. Under Pluto's tutelage they will eventually make the choice between their overriding ambition and the compulsion to find satisfying expression of their emotionality in close relationships.

These individuals have many paths from which to choose. The Libran ascendent suggests areas where color, line, proportion and texture would be important. Interior decoration, architecture or fabric and clothes design would utilize these talents effectively. Politics, government positions, public works administration or consumerism would be excellent fields for their prowess. They may possibly prefer a profession which would allow them to practice at home. Whatever they select they will persevere until they reach the pinnacle where they can shout to the world, "Look at me now! I made it!"

PEOPLE BORN WITH PLUTO IN CANCER IN THE TENTH HOUSE

1. Betty Ford, former First Lady:[2] April 8, 1918, 3:26 p.m. CST, Chicago, Illinois.

2. Ann Landers and Abigail Van Buren (twins), columnists:[2] July 4, 1918, 10:01 a.m. and 10:09 a.m. CWT, respectively, Sioux City, Iowa.
3. Barbara Walters, news correspondent:[13] September 25, 1931, 6:50 a.m. EST, Boston, Massachusetts.
4. Elizabeth Taylor, actress:[3] February 27, 1932, 7:56 p.m. GMT, London, England.
5. Shirley MacLaine, actress:[3] April 24, 1934, 3:57 p.m. EST, Richmond, Virginia.

PLUTO IN CANCER IN THE ELEVENTH HOUSE

In the Aquarian house of friendship, these natives will feel deeply about emotional ties with others. They will mother their friends or expect mothering from them. At times, it will be difficult to distinguish which tendency they are manifesting. They may go to extremes in giving of themselves, and expect in return some kind of emotional slavery. Others may run their lives for them, exercising too much control and domininating them entirely.

With Virgo on the ascendent, the ability to be discriminating in close relationships, to pick and choose one's friends wisely after lengthy exposure to their characters, can be used in a positive way to prevent such undesirable results.

Friends, to them, are family and will always be treated with hospitality and warmly welcomed into the home. Likewise, they will expect to be considered as one of the family in return. The eleventh house represents our capacity to receive love and here it is powerfully expressed. Sometime in their lives the Pluto regenerational force will affect them. Then they will prune out those friendships which are no longer necessary or satisfying in their search for growth.

It is an interesting sidelight, on the Pluto in Cancer placement, to note the activities and compositions of the numerous men's community service clubs: the Lions, Rotarians, Elks, Kiwanis, Shriners. Memberships in these groups are composed primarily of Pluto-in-Cancer men who organize and expend their energies on a practical level in helping the blind, the handicapped, the unfortunates of our society. This is truly a Cancerian response working through a positive productive outlet.

PEOPLE BORN WITH PLUTO IN CANCER IN THE ELEVENTH HOUSE

1. John Mitchell, former Attorney General:[1 3] September 5, 1913, 3:30 a.m. EST, Detroit, Michigan.
2. Leonard Bernstein, composer, conductor:[3] August 25, 1918, 6:06 a.m. EDT, Lawrence, Massachusetts.
3. Henry Louis "Hank" Aaron, baseball player:[2] February 5, 1934, 7:45 p.m. CST, Mobile, Alabama.

4. Joan Kennedy, wife of Edward Kennedy:[13] September 5, 1936, 6:10 a.m. EDT, New York, New York.
5. Dick Cavett, TV talk show host:[3] November 19, 1936, 1:24 a.m. CST, Kearney, Nebraska.

PLUTO IN CANCER IN THE TWELFTH HOUSE

Pluto in Cancer in the twelfth sets off the trine of water signs in the water houses; Scorpio on the cusp of the fourth and Pisces on the cusp of the eighth. Consider then the natural rulers of these houses: Neptune in the twelfth, the Moon in the fourth, and Pluto in the eighth. All three signs are flavored with Cancer, Scorpio and Pisces and, likewise, the Moon, Pluto and Neptune. It is obvious in this situation that there is a strong interplay and interdependency, somewhat like a three-way mutual reception. In this chart, all of the emotional and intuitive feelings are powerful and flow freely. The natives are psychic sponges, constantly absorbing the vibrations of those around them.

The presence of Pluto in the twelfth arouses the natives' desire to plumb the depths and understand the self. Cancer holds tenaciously to memories. This clutching, this unwillingness to let go may become an obsession. Here a finely drawn line distinguishes what is healthy to discard and what is unhealthy to keep. If they permit themselves to cling to bitter and painful memories, allowing them to fester in their unconscious mind, they can trap themselves in the past and be forever lost in a Neptunian world of self-delusion. They need to look for a balance between the past and the present. Sometime in their lives, when the natal Pluto is triggered, they will search within to discover what must be uprooted and discarded in order to experience renewal and rebirth and find fulfillment on the path to successful living. This is indeed a heavy burden to bear. If they are unable to accomplish this weeding out, they may end up prisoners of their own negative psychic expressions, totally withdrawn from the world.

The fourth house Scorpio influence manifests in the natives' desire to understand their roots. They are curious about their backgrounds: "Where did I come from? What have I inherited from my family? What racial strains flow through my blood stream?" They become aware of the physical attributes of their parents: their build, coloring, speech and posture. They yearn to comprehend the complexities of their parents and the circumstances that have shaped them. Only then, when they have reached this understanding, do they know that from the depths of the twelfth house, these subtle powers have crystallized to create the individual who springs forth from the first.

The Pisces eighth house influence activates the natives' need to search into the unknown, focusing on the occult, psychic phenomena and research in these areas. Pluto urges the investigation of truth and the tearing away of the Neptunian veil of illusion. In this search they will eventually discover their own Scorpio code by which it is practical and possible for them to function.

To sum up the powerful urges at work here, the natives are given the unparalled opportunity to marshal their emotions and psychic feelings into a potent force for the understanding of self and mankind.

PEOPLE BORN WITH PLUTO IN CANCER IN THE TWELFTH HOUSE

1. George Wallace, former Governor of Alabama:[2] August 25, 1919, 3:30 a.m., Clio, Alabama.
2. Judy Garland, actress and singer:[3] June 10, 1922, 6:00 a.m. CST, Grand Rapids, Michigan.
3. Marilyn Monroe, actress:[6] June 1, 1926, 9:30 a.m. PST, Los Angeles, California.
4. H. R. Haldemann, former assistant to President Nixon:[13] October 27, 1926, 3:30 a.m. PST, Los Angeles, California.
5. Edmund G. Brown, Governor of California:[5] April 7, 1938, 12:34 p.m. PST, San Francisco, California.

CHAPTER TWO
PLUTO IN LEO

TO PLUTO IN LEO
THE WAYS

To every man there openeth
A Way, and Ways, and a Way.
And the High Soul climbs the High Way.
And the Low Soul gropes the Low,
And in between on the misty flats
The rest drift to and fro.
But to every man there openeth
A High Way, and a Low;
And every man decideth
The Way his soul shall go.

–John Oxenham

THE GENERATIONAL INFLUENCES

October 8, 1937 to November 15, 1937; August 5, 1938 to February 7, 1939; June 15, 1939 to October 19, 1956; January 16, 1957 to August 18, 1957.

The impact of Pluto in the sign of Leo, from 1938 to 1957, defined itself in a generation that sought openly for self-expression. The individual was king, with all the monarch's privileges at his command. The unrestricted flow of energies and desires was extremely important in the unfolding of the personality. The Leo aristocrat, wearing nobility dramatically like a stage costume, merged somewhat uneasily with the Scorpio plutocrat who exuded the aura of money and rank. A powerful individual strode forth to leave its mark unmistakably on the world.

The tremendous Leo ego bursting forth here must first be tempered and contained within reasonable Scorpio limits; it must of necessity die before it can be reborn; and it must extinguish its burning fires before it can be rekindled to warm the world. Reflecting back over the recent past, we can see where this has already happened. This vital generation which came of age in the turbulent Sixties, leaving an indelible mark upon the pages of history, is now experiencing the transit of Pluto through Libra, sextiling all natal placements. A greater understanding of the power of peace, justice and equality has descended upon millions of these young people. Instead of trying by violent means to force their revolutionary demands on the populace, they have adjusted to more conventional and lawful ways of change. They are now back in the establishment working with it, instead of against it.

This generation was conceived by Pluto-in-Cancer parents who wished, first of all, to give their children everything they had been deprived of during the strict upbringing of the Twenties and the financial deprivation of the Thirties. The freedom to come and go as they wished with no responsibilities was theirs for the asking. The resounding cry, "I want it better for my child than it was for me," swept over the nation. And so they had it all—tricycles, bicycles, Chevy coupes, weekly allowances for movies and sodas, summer camp, prepaid college tuition and fun, fun, fun.

Family disciplines were relaxed; the teenager as a distinct sociological species burst into bloom, occupying the rumpus room with friends and monopolizing the phone. Manufacturers churned out records, clothes, movies and magazines catering to the tremendous mass market comprised of the group with money in its pockets and the eagerness to spend it. Rock and roll music, accompanied by the Twist, erupted on the national scene and changed forever the course of popular music and dancing. Ubiquitous American youth seized the center of the stage.

The Pluto-in-Cancer father, reacting to the restraints of his adolescence, decided to lower the barriers and become a pal to his children. He joined them in their sports and games, peppered his conversation with their slang and laughed indulgently at their antics. Meanwhile, he worried secretly about paying the bills for all their happy activities.

During this period, the Pluto-in-Cancer mother, who had been reared in a sheltered environment, entered the work force, in many cases for the first time. Spurred on by patriotism during World War II she filled a variety of jobs in replacing the men called into the service. After discovering that she enjoyed the feeling of independence and earning her own money she often preferred to remain employed. The revitalized post-war economy, geared to tempt the luxury-starved customer, created many new fascinating gadgets and appliances. Her pay check helped to buy the bigger refigerator, the second car, the third television set.

To compensate for her failure as a full-time mother she showered her children with possessions to keep them happy, but, at the same time, was filled with guilt. Inwardly she felt that she was failing to fulfill the type-cast role remembered from her youth. If she wasn't in the kitchen preparing dinner when the kids came home, they could reach her down at the office or in the electronics plant and, of course, they were always free to invite their friends over to loll around the rumpus room and play their latest records. Rarely did she expect them to carry out mundane chores—making their beds, washing dishes, putting out the trash–duties which she had performed so diligently in her childhood. She wanted them to be free of responsibilities and to have a good time.

And how did this affect the children born with Pluto in Leo? In true Leo fashion, they expected the world on a platter and saw no reason why life's pleasures should be denied them. It was their right to enjoy, to experience, to play their games and flower in the sun. Rich or poor, educated or not, whatever income level they were plugged in to, they anticipated–and usually got–the best their parents could give them. And these hardworking parents stood on the sidelines delighted to indulge their every whim.

Those who trudged off to college in the placid fifties treated the occasion as a happy social event. To the young women the campus was a courting ground where they stalked their prey with a practiced eye, taking in the young man's appearance, family background, financial standing and possible money-making abilities. These women were aware of society's intense pressures to get married before they reached their middle twenties or consider themselves relegated to the human scrap heap.

The young men expected college to be a playground with an endless round of parties and sports in which they would naturally excel. If they took their studies seriously (and many did, of course) they concealed it carefully behind a facade of gaiety and good humor. Armed with youth and health, Chevy convertibles, stunning wardrobes, cases of beer and enough of the old man's money to pay the tuition, they did indeed have the world on a string.

The movies of the times, which they faithfully attended, saturated them with love stories wallowing in romanticism, cardboard characters and happy endings. The handsome hero and the beautiful heroine, after painfully enduring the conflicts of predictable plots, merged into a passionate embrace, shown from the neck up, and with their hair perfectly groomed and makeup intact, took off for the M.G.M. horizon in a rosy haze. The audience was left with the impression that the rosy haze lasted a lifetime, and they never had so much as a cross word. All of this nonsense, as delightful and escapist as it was at the time, did not prepare these young people for the realities of everyday marriage. Later on, many relationships floundered and sank because the principals subconsciously expected their partner to be Lana Turner or Clark Gable with every hair in place at 7:30 in the morning.

The Pluto-in-Leo natives born in the late Forties and Fifties are the segment of our society which broke all the rules and made shocking headlines in the tumultuous Sixties. They have indeed left their mark on history.

As this generation matured, the familiar luxuries of their younger years no longer seemed as important or exciting. They became aware of their parents struggle for security and status, the better job, the newer car, the bigger house. They observed also how their parents were formed in a rigid conservative mold, unable to alter their behavior, seeking constantly to please, to placate their children, to smooth away any rough edges in daily living, to turn away from any unpleasantness and hastily stuff it into the closet. Their credo had always been that if there was enough money in the bank to cover any emergencies nothing could go wrong. Or could it?

So the young people, having been surfeited with possessions and having observed that they did not insure a happy life, found themselves groping and reaching out for other disciplines and ideologies. What else was out there in the mainstream of life? How were they to use the Leo force? Slowly but surely, in a rising crescendo, the Plutonian power of a whole generation was unleashed on a startled world.

They rebelled first against the senseless slaughter of the Viet Nam conflict. Thousands of young men of draft age refused to be swept into the armed forces to fight a war halfway across the world. They were in the prime of life and they were not about to die on some foreign battlefied for some unknown cause. Many who believed passionately in the right to their own destiny forsook their American citizenship and sought refuge in other countries.

With the tragic murder of President Kennedy they mourned the loss of a kindred spirit. He had been young and vital and he had understood them. Now he was gone and the American dream would never be the same.

While continuing their thunderous protests against the war, they took up the crusade for the rights of black people and other minorities, forcing their hidebound elders to face the issue of discrimination squarely. They spread violence and disruption on college and university campuses in passionate revolt against the outmoded concepts of education. They brought sexuality out of the closet, treating it with refreshing frankness and honesty, and along the way, inaugurated the practice of a man and woman living openly together without benefit of marriage.

They shook their Pluto-in-Cancer parents to the roots in their outright rejection of the old value system. Everything came up for review: the sanctity of the home, parental respect, higher education, the worship of the great god Success—and all were dramatically and deliberately reviled. They didn't value a home; home was anywhere they dropped their sleeping bags. They didn't respect parents who didn't respect them as individuals. They didn't want a college degree if all it fitted them for was a slot in the establishment and the inevitable pressure-cooker existence.

The young women, in their own way, after taking a hard, calculating look around, renounced the typical mother-wife role which had survived for so long. They were seeking more out of life than what had been dealt to their mothers: an endless round of housework and child rearing sandwiched in between a dull routine job in the business world and the chance to play servant and second-class citizen to an insensitive clod of a husband. It was going to be quite different for them. No man was going to own them and keep them subservient to his desires. In the lingo of the era, they sought to find themselves, to express their talents freely and to seek their own special niche in the outside world.

In hot-headed rebellion, many of these youths left the security of their homes to hitch-hike across the country. They lived mainly by their wits, scrounging sleeping places, food and now and then, jobs. Some retired to communes to live off the land, forsaking overstocked refrigerators and workable plumbing. Others chose to find new worlds to conquer by traveling overseas to teach the natives of underprivileged countries about crop rotation and soil management.

In massive defiance against dead-end materialism, many retreated totally and were forever lost in a mindless world of drugs and sexual debauchery. With transiting Neptune squaring the natal Leo placement during this period they drifted easily into a private place of fantasy and illusion, escaping from the pressures of daily existence and finding release only in death.

Through all of the tragedy and upheaval, Pluto was working in subtle and hidden ways. Now in the late Seventies, we can look back on this period and realize that a great deal of lasting good emerged from the rubble. Many antiquated values were burned up or washed away as the Leo and Pluto energies coalesced.

This generation has chosen some remarkable life styles as they harness their creative forces in a positive way. Many who would have ordinarily been part of the corporate structure elected to merge into the blue collar class and work with their hands and the strength of their bodies as well as their minds. In our tightly woven, interdependent civilization, they are well aware that the men who keep the electricity flowing, the roads paved and the telephone system functioning are making paramount contributions to our daily lives. The social stigma of the blue collar has disappeared and the wearer is no longer considered inferior to the gentleman with the attache case.

In direct contradiction to the huge conglomerates that were gobbling up enormous sections of American industry, many young people chose instead to make friends with their local Chamber of Commerce and shake hands briefly with the I.R.S., as they pooled their money and talent and poured it into small businesses. The populace was drawn to these entrepreneurs who offered enthusiasm and personal service instead of bored looks from behind the counters of their stores. The Leo urge to create manifested in small restaurants offering home-made delights, in bookstores crammed with fascinating paperbacks and in small specialty shops displaying handcrafted articles made with distinction and loving care.

Those who remain in the business, professional and political arenas pursue their careers with greater comprehension of the fundamental rights of all. Not satisfied any longer with stereotypes and routine procedures they are grappling with new and dramatic solutions to man's eternal problems. Pluto has dug it up, now Leo is hauling it out in the sunshine to look at it squarely, dusting off the cobwebs to see how the machinery of all the arts and sciences can be used for the good of all.

Millions of them, including many members of minority groups, have attended college, are still attending, and in some cases plan never to stop. They are by far the most highly educated single group contributing to our culture. All those degrees and all that knowledge must ultimately work towards the betterment of mankind.

They will freely admit, with their customary candor, that money and comfort are important to them. But unlike their parents who strove for possessions and bank accounts as a badge of security and status, they are satisfied at present with a modest car, a workable television set and a clean apartment. They will tell you rather proudly that their badge of security is themselves. The lusting after power has been tempered with the Plutonian experience and rebirth that millions of them have undergone.

From front stage center, the Pluto-in-Leo generation has dramatically demanded of us all to be tolerant of the other's point of view, to challenge hypocrisy and drag it out into the light, to appreciate the worth of the individual, to have honesty of purpose and to treat man-woman relationships with disarming candor.

May they continue to use their great ability for effective leadership in its most positive manifestations.

PLUTO IN LEO SQUARE PLUTO'S NATURAL HOUSE

Pluto in Leo brings about the inner tensions resulting from a planet ruling a water sign positioned in a fire sign. Here, Pluto's water can extinguish Leo's abundant fire, or Leo's fire can contain Pluto's water, causing it to evaporate and turn into steam. If these forces are not used wisely, they can nullify the best qualities of each.

Basically, the struggle exists between emotion and will. These individuals need both attributes in their search to develop themselves fully as human beings. It is necessary for them to understand and come to terms with the inner conflicts that this placement brings about. Unless these energies are used wisely, the dangers of egotism and power can disrupt their lives.

Furthermore, Scorpio is in square aspect to the Leo house throughout the following twelve delineations. A grand cross in the fixed signs of Taurus, Leo, Scorpio and Aquarius is created. When Leo appears in an angular house, the first, fourth, seventh, and tenth, the cardinal expression will be intermingled with the fixity. Yet the fact that the signs are in cardinal houses gives the native the opportunity to solve these dilemmas, because cardinal houses stir one into positive action.

When all four signs fall in fixed houses, the second, fifth, eighth and eleventh, the fixity will be keenly felt. The individuals will not want to change; they will dredge up every ounce of stubborn, hard-headed resistance, banging their heads against the wall, but change they will not. If they do not learn to bend and adjust to life's variations like the tree in the storm, they may end up being literally broken.

When the four fixed signs mark cadent houses, the third, sixth, ninth and twelfth, the situation becomes easier to handle. They are more flexible in the nature of cadent houses. These will bend naturally with the forces that overtake them and in so doing will accommodate the changes occurring in their lives.

In this placement, the astrologer must take extraordinary care in counseling the client for he or she is faced with the condition of the super ego: the total absorption in the emotional self. These individuals dislike being told they have a tremendous ego because seldom, if ever, can they easily admit it is so. They carry all their ego-eggs in one basket, up front and on view, and are not willing to unload them and scatter them around in other baskets, eliminating the risk of all breaking at once. They cannot see life from any perspective but their own. They must be consciously aware of this total absorption before they can change their ways and temper these giant forces within. Water must flow freely or it becomes stagnant. Fire must be wisely controlled or it will burn.

PLUTO IN LEO THROUGH THE HOUSES

In an effort to help the reader apply the Pluto interpretations presented in this book, we are listing the degrees of importance that Pluto in Leo assumes when found in the following situations:

1. Pluto is most powerful when the natal Sun is in Scorpio or when there is a stellium in Scorpio.
2. Pluto is powerful when it is in Leo's natural fifth house, or in its own natural eighth house.
3. The power of Pluto is intensified if it is conjunct the Sun in Leo.
4. If Pluto is square the Sun in Taurus, the difficulties will be felt strongly in the fundamental ego drives of the native. If Pluto is square the Sun in Scorpio, a mutual reception exists, creating harmony and softening the tension of the square.
5. If Pluto is opposite the Sun in Aquarius, a seesaw effect of dependency or independence must be resolved and the forces joined together in a compromise.
6. If Pluto is trine the Sun in Aries or Sagittarius, the basic drives will be easily expressed.
7. If Pluto is sextile the Sun in Gemini or Libra,

an opportunity for growth is present in the houses governed by these signs.

8. If Pluto is quincunx the Sun in Capricorn or Pisces, tension and strain result because the two planets are not in the same element and are uncomfortable with each other. Often a health aspect is involved.

9. If Pluto is semisextile the Sun in Cancer or Virgo, no special interplay occurs. It is a neutral aspect.

PLUTO IN LEO IN THE FIRST HOUSE

Those with Pluto in Leo in the first house project themselves into their sphere with an air of authority that can be wondrous to behold. Here is self-will at its height: strong, determined, and stubborn. They are out to prove unmistakably to the world that they are indeed Number One. Do not doubt them for a minute.

A quality of leadership emanates with such power that others may be immediately drawn to them, becoming devoted and adoring slaves. They have the ability to inspire others to follow them anywhere in all manner of crusades; for religious, political or pleasurable reasons. The Plutonian struggle is dramatized by the uses of this power; for the greater good of mankind or for self-gratification. Negatively, they can become tyrants, basking in self-glory, seeking to control and use others for selfish ends. Positively, they can be leaders who inspire the multitudes towards better lives.

With Scorpio on the fourth, they may have been dominated by a parent in youth. Such domination could have affected them in two ways. Their security may have been threatened and as they mature they may compensate in a headstrong drive to tell the world from Aries natural house, "I am." If, on the other hand, parental overindulgence has turned them into spoiled brats, they will react by accepting the position of king of the household as their rightful due and spend their days ruthlessly demanding that which they crave. It will not matter whether they were born into a rich or poor family background. The Leo qualities lead them to expect that they will possess the best of everything.

The Capricorn inconjunct accents the health aspect of the placement. The native must learn to bend, literally, from the knees in reverence to a higher force than themselves. They must exercise in order to use their bodies with ease and fluidity. If they do not, they may suffer from chronic ailments brought about by rigidity and laziness.

The Pluto regeneration will manifest in the natives' experience of learning to wield the power within themselves, to control the self and not the rest of the environment. Once this is accomplished they will find their pathway to achievement less burdensome and ultimately, more fulfilling.

In the native's appearance, the crowning glory of Leo, the thick mane of hair, will be noticeable. The body is broadshouldered and well-proportioned. They walk with a leonine stride; graceful, lithesome and free.

PEOPLE BORN WITH PLUTO IN LEO IN THE FIRST HOUSE

1. Lily Tomlin, comedienne:[13] September 1, 1939, 1:45 a.m. EST, Detroit, Michigan.
2. James Caan, actor:[13] March 26, 1940, 12:45 p.m. EST, Bronx, New York.
3. Bobby Fischer, chess champion:[3] March 9, 1943, 2:39 p.m. CDT, Chicago, Illinois.
4. Prince Charles of England, British Royal Family:[12] November 14, 1948, 9:14 p.m. GMT, London, England.

PLUTO IN LEO IN THE SECOND HOUSE

Here in Taurus' house Venusian values are interwoven with self and one's pleasures. The natives may be obsessed with the security that possessions give them, always wanting more than they have already acquired, something bigger and better to add to their accumulation of things. They search eagerly, spending freely on glittering trinkets and shiny objects as well as huge hunks of land, race horses and yachts. It is difficult for them to distinguish quality from quantity as they gamble openly on both love affairs and business deals.

With the Cancer sensitivity in the first and the Scorpio intensity in the fifth their emotions will be shackled until they undergo the Plutonian regeneration in their acceptance of the basic and lasting values of life, and then discover their own self worth. They have a heartfelt need for romantic love and until this urge is fulfilled they will feel lonely and apart. Quite often Leo is playacting. Love does not come easily—not until they are able to go beyond artificiality and learn to love themselves for the right reasons. They must also learn that everyone does not have to bow down to them and declare devotion, for not all will be their admiring subjects. When they finally experience this transformation, they will be able to reach out with warmth and generosity for the love and affection of others.

PEOPLE BORN WITH PLUTO IN LEO IN THE SECOND HOUSE

1. Lee Harvey Oswald, murderer of President John F. Kennedy:[6] October 18, 1939, 9:55 p.m. CST, New Orleans, Louisiana.
2. Ryan O'Neill, actor:[6] April 20, 1941, 9:34 a.m. PST, Los Angeles, California.
3. Patricia Nixon Cox, daughter of Richard M. Nixon:[6] February 21, 1946, 1:37 p.m. PST, Whittier, California.

4. Farrah Fawcett Majors, model, TV star:[5] February 2, 1947, 3:10 p.m. CST, Corpus Christi, Texas.
5. John Travolta, actor:[13] June 13, 1951, 5:00 a.m. EDT, New York, New York.

PLUTO IN LEO IN THE THIRD HOUSE

With Gemini on the ascendent and Pluto in Gemini's house, those who deal with the power of communication step forth. They tell fascinating stories, dramatize their daily activities, buttonhole their friends to entertain them with their latest adventures. This torrent of words will be liberally spiced with humor and tinged with a show-business flair.

But tension arises between Leo's need to be openly self-expressive and Pluto's desire to hold everything inside until they are sure of themselves. Thus, these individuals seek knowledge at an early age, keeping it to themselves, and as they mature and the Pluto experience takes hold they are then able to voice their fervent emotions with assurance and sincerity. They want to have pride in their ability to speak honestly and openly.

Scorpio in the sixth may intensify negative traits. Individuals with this placement may become bombastic, overbearing and bitingly sarcastic in speech. The square, boomeranging from the sixth, needs release and unless the natives can find it in a satisfying and creative outlet, their health and popularity may be affected. Nervous tension or problems with internal organs could result.

In their speech they can cut sharply to the core of the matter, laying it bare in one swift stroke. They can sniff out falsehoods and mercilessly expose them. They may be intolerant and impatient of others in their lack of skill in expressing their ideas, but once they acknowledge this trait in themselves, they may learn patience and allow others to speak their piece.

Writing science fiction or ghost stories is an excellent choice in using these abilities. They would also be extremely capable and find positive delight in writing about their own exploits. By channeling their verbal talents they would make fine actors or directors in any form of the theatre arts.

PEOPLE BORN WITH PLUTO IN LEO IN THE THIRD HOUSE

1. John Denver, singer, lyricist, composer:[6] December 21, 1943, 3:55 p.m. MWT, Roswell, New Mexico.
2. Richard Thomas, actor:[11] June 13, 1951, 5:00 a.m. EDT, New York, New York.

PLUTO IN LEO IN THE FOURTH HOUSE

One of the overdone and trite meanings of this placement is the native who yearns for and eventually gets the house on the hill. Then the Leo personality can gaze down with paternal benevolence upon the poor peasants milling around below who are looking up in awestruck wonder at this fine castle. In our present day life style, it is perhaps clearer to substitute for the castle, the palatial cliff-house hanging out over the ocean and change the peasants into middle class families inhabiting similar boxlike structures in suburbia.

To complement this picture, the Leo host or hostess enjoys dispensing entertainment, delicious food and generous drinks with a lavish hand to all their subjects lucky enough to be invited into the castle. From the security of this bastion, they are indeed the king and queen. Underneath the surface frivolity, however, they tackle party-giving as a serious affair.

In solemn moments these natives retreat into their home for self-regeneration. Eventually their search will uncover the proper perspective on their inclination to play king. Here they are secure against the tensions and strains of the battle for survival in the everyday world. It is their haven of peace, the inner-sanctum of their souls.

The fourth house influence of roots and beginnings is extremely strong with Pluto in Cancer's house. Their desire for their own home even in youth will challenge them to pursue this goal throughout their lives. They express pride in family lineage in various ways; the family tree illustrated in a large, handsomely decorated chart, the family crest displayed on the wall, or, reaching the ultimate, an ancient suit of armor standing in the hall.

The natives' lesson in this placement may lie in the confusion experienced in selecting a partner. In early years, before they fully understood the Pluto forces, they may choose a mate for surface motives only, purely for his or her ability to complement the royal role. The other necessary ingredients for a good marriage—love, respect, understanding, good communication, common interests—may be lacking. As they mature they eventually realize they made their choice for the wrong reasons. When it becomes apparent that this regal personage does not fulfill their emotional needs, they will then seek out the right partner, not for the social or financial register, but for the register in their heart.

PEOPLE BORN WITH PLUTO IN LEO IN THE FOURTH HOUSE

1. Joan Baez, folk singer:[2] January 9, 1941, 11:50 a.m. EST, New York, New York.
2. Wayne Newton, singer:[6] April 3, 1942, 8:22 a.m. EWT, Norfolk, Virginia.
3. Angela Davis, political activist:[2] January 26, 1944, 12:30 p.m. CDT, Birmingham, Alabama.
4. Liza Minnelli, singer, actress, daughter of Judy

Garland:[3] March 12, 1946, 7:58 a.m. PST, Los Angeles, California.

5. Christine Onassis, daughter of Aristotle Onassis:[5] December 11, 1950, 3:00 p.m. EST, New York, New York.

PLUTO IN LEO IN THE FIFTH HOUSE

A powerful square is created here with Leo in its own house and Taurus, Scorpio and Aquarius in theirs; fixed signs in fixed houses. The Pluto energies intensify, seeking release in affectional relationships with children, sexual involvements, artistic pursuits and speculative ventures.

In love affairs these natives can exhibit such rampant charm and romanticism that those they pursue may find it almost impossible to turn them away. The slightest discouragement will cause them to increase their efforts. Here is the Don Juan of the Zodiac flitting from one erotic entanglement to another. Inside, they simmer with an almost unhealthy need to have everyone love them. When inevitably they experience rejection they slink away to their private lair, licking their wounded Leo pride. Cynicism, self-doubt and moodiness may cast gloom on their usual sunny dispositions. But after a period of introspection they bounce back into the arena to continue their amorous conquests and "show them all."

Only when the Scorpio eighth house pressure

for regeneration and renewal is consciously dredged up, will these souls learn to handle these vital forces in a positive way. They must recognize the sensitivity and individuality of the other person as being equal to, but perhaps different from, their own. They cannot find true happiness in attempting to dominate their will, their love expression, their inner being. Once again they must learn that not everybody in the world is going to love them. If they eventually discover the one person they care for deeply, who can truly love them for themselves, they will indeed be fortunate.

With their children they are hard taskmasters. Their Leo vanity expects impeccable behavior from them at all times. Otherwise, what will the neighbors think if they do not conduct themselves like little kings and queens? The children are not only their creations but counterparts of their own personality. They may brag about their triumphs: the lead role in a little theatre group or the blue ribbon won at a sports event, but they will remain silent about their children's expertise in washing dishes or stacking up the trash. Only when high standards are met will these parents openly express their love and affection. Because they are looking for a reflection of the king within themselves, they may be too demanding. In turn the children, feeling that they are rejected because of the parents' impossible standards, may withhold their affection. The parents need this vital sustenance to grow and expand in their lives but only when they realize that the children are unique individuals apart from their own selves will the relationship between them fully blossom.

One of their strongest needs is the desire for self-expression. In some ways their children may be their self-expression, but too much of this can be harmful. They will find greater fulfillment in working with them in sports activities where their natural sunny leadership and love of the outdoors will be an advantage. Also, involvement in amateur theatre projects or hobbies of various kinds would be an excellent answer. The renewal forces are working here to demand that they alter their focus of attention from themselves into active participation with others in creative projects.

Their natural interest in speculation and outdoor sports requires controlled expression. However, if they allow the Leo gambling instinct and the Pluto lust for power to override common sense they can gallop away on a thoroughbred horse in hot pursuit of the elusive pot of gold. They may find the pot of gold, perhaps, but discover that the pot has rusted and the gold doesn't buy what they really want. They should never use joint resources in wild speculative ventures. That way lies chaos. The physical drives sweeping through the fifth house must be channeled into constructive uses or these individuals may rush headlong into disaster.

Since this is a fixed square, the native will find it extremely difficult to break the habits of the past. Scorpio in its own house and squaring the Leo placement may bring about such stress that these individuals will be forced to unlock their eighth house secrets of rebirth and renewal, and apply them through deep study and introspection to their own character. They must combine the Leo pride and the Scorpio conservatism in emotional harmony so that both aspects can work freely.

The subtlety of Pluto will surface in their increasing awareness of the rights and privileges of others, who quite often are out there in the arena bleeding from the heart. Once these truths are embraced, these natives will be able to harness the Leo and Scorpio energies for their ultimate peace of mind in fruitful relationships with those they love.

PEOPLE BORN WITH PLUTO IN LEO IN THE FIFTH HOUSE

1. Ringo Starr, singer, composer, one of the Beatles:[3] July 7, 1940, 00:01 a.m. GDT, Liverpool, England.
2. Barbra Streisand, singer, actress:[3] April 24, 1942, 5:16 a.m. EWT, Brooklyn, New York.
3. Cheryl Crane, murderess, daughter of Lana Turner:[6] July 25, 1943, 11:26 p.m. PWT, Los Angeles, California.
4. Sandy Duncan, actress:[1] February 20, 1946, 8:00 a.m. CST, Henderson, Texas.

PLUTO IN LEO IN THE SIXTH HOUSE

The basic conflict here arises from the nature of the two signs, Leo in Virgo's natural house. Leo projects warmly, openly, ardently. Virgo is intrinsically shy, timid, cool. Leo demands the limelight. Virgo runs for cover. Here the Leo king is uncomfortable in the house of the servant. Discord results over the need to serve, but how? What method is fit for the king?

The Leo characteristics may break out in domination of others who inhabit their workaday world. They can be patronizing, looking down in haughty grandeur from their invisible throne; or, they can perform service in such subtle ways that they are saying, in effect, "I'm helping you, but what's in it for me?" They naturally assume that it is unnecessary to start on the bottom rung of the corporate ladder in their climb to the top. For them there is no bottom rung. They anticipate that their sterling worth will be recognized shortly by the powers-that-be who will then delegate them to their rightful position as chief of operations. Nor do they need to be instructed in their duties. They already know exactly what they are and how they are going to execute them. None of these attitudes is going to endear them to their fellow workers.

With Scorpio on the cusp of the ninth the Plutonian renewal will be intermingled with the search for wisdom and learning. Sometimes their searing emotional experiences and bitter disappointments will teach them more than any book ever can. Once they realize that the Leo pride and arrogance are not making any friends, then hopefully they will turn to the other facets of their character—the desire to bring warmth and comfort to others. If they wish ardently to be of service, they must first learn how to talk with, and relate to, other people and develop a philosophy of life in tune with their levels.

In career matters they have many fine choices. Scorpios make excellent surgeons because they often instinctively know where to cut the body open for the best possible results. Because of Pluto's thrust, they are often invested with the facility and skill to plumb the depths of emotional forces in others. This talent would be invaluable in the fields of psychology, psychiatry and other forms of counseling. They would also function well in on-the-job training programs which give them the opportunity to combine the Leo dramatics with the Virgo teaching skills.

No matter what they choose to do, the danger exists that they may become obsessed with their work. The rest of the world may cease to exist for them as they bury their heads in the daily grind. If they come to an impasse in the extraordinary urge to regenerate their work life, they may turn into hypochondriacs, boring everyone with a detailed recital of all their bodily aches and pains. Or illness may erupt in any cf the areas ruled by Leo, Scorpio and Sagittarius. Pluto is warning them to eliminate all the negative factors in the sixth house sector. If regeneration does not eventually take place, they will suffer in both the areas of work and health.

PEOPLE BORN WITH PLUTO IN LEO IN THE SIXTH HOUSE

1. Janis Joplin, rock singer:[3] January 19, 1943, 9:45 a.m. CDT, Port Arthur, Texas.
2. Joe Namath, football player:[6] May 31, 1943, 00:30 a.m. EST, Beaver Falls, Pennsylvania.
3. Julie Kavner, actress:[6] September 7, 1950, 6:45 p.m. PDT, Los Angeles, California.
4. Princess Caroline of Monaco, Monaco Royal Family:[12] January 23, 1957, 9:27 a.m., Monte Carlo.

PLUTO IN LEO IN THE SEVENTH HOUSE

Again, the unusual situation involving the four elements, this time in cardinal houses, arises. Leo's fire is in Libra's airy house, while watery Scorpio, ruled by Pluto, is on the cusp of Saturn's earth house. Air feeds fire; water feeds earth. This fortunate interplay helps to alleviate the impact of the Leo-Scorpio square in the angles. Also, the potential exists to maintain a well-balanced area of life, in seventh house matters, primarily in relationship to others. Earth adds practicality, water pours out feeling, fire sparks enthusiasm and drive, and air contributes mental and intellectual leverage. Within these individuals lies the ability to structure and consolidate personal energies, releasing them to the world in a positive direction.

In Libra's house, however, these natives wrestle with two opposite forces: the desire for a sense of equality and fairness in the marriage and the desire to dominate the partner before the partner dominates them. Obviously, they cannot have both equality and domination.

With the fixed square in angular houses, accenting the Taurus-Scorpio polarity from the fourth to the tenth, they may at first be affected by strong parental influences, most likely from the mother. If she was a vital, overwhelming personality who controlled the life in early years, the natives may long to break away from such threats on reaching maturity. They may unconsciously search for a partner that can be manipulated in order to achieve a balance; or they may attract another strong person who will continue the domination started by the mother. Much time may be spent in intellectual analysis of this problem. The Leo fire can be fanned into greater strength by the Libra air, or the Libra air can contain and blow out the fire. They find it difficult to attain what they really want because in this case, they do not know. They may see in all members of the opposite sex the craving to be in command. Either way the Plutonian force will hold sway. Will they be the leader in the relationship and wield iron-handed control or will the other individual force them to maintain their dependency? It is indeed a dilemma and the Libran trait of indecision does not allow for an easy answer. The native may go through two or three marriages before finding a comfortable solution.

Sometime in the life their pride may be brought up short as they are forced to confront their crumbling relationships. Since they constantly want approval for themselves, they may finally become consciously aware that there must be some reason why their love affairs end in unhappiness. One of their loved ones might blurt out in a moment of anger that the king's role of tyrant is too much to endure. The king can reign over his subjects for a long time before they later rebel, but when they do rebel they drag him down from the throne to take his place alongside everyone else. Pluto dredges up these faults for contemplation and ultimately demands that the native reestablish and rejuvenate partnerships, cleaning out the castle and burning up the debris, and along the way learn what equality really means by putting it into practice. Then their lives will be richly rewarded in affections and love for others and they will be able to release their glorious Leo tendencies of generosity and warmth of feeling.

Considering the stabilizing influence of Scorpio on the cusp of Saturn's house this placement is excellent for a husband and wife working together in a business partnership. The arrangement, however, must be based on true sharing, a fine balance of responsibilities.

It is also important for the native to select a partner for the right reasons, because of love, and not because the partner was born in a high zoning area. True love doesn't come attached to status and riches.

The Scorpio authority from the tenth and the subsequent fixed desire to achieve in the world, may delay these natives' search for a mate. They feel they must first get to the top before they can seek marriage. To them, their worldly position has a direct bearing on the success of their intimate relationships. They must succeed first, and when this has been accomplished and they enter into the marriage state, the partner must work in harmony to further their success.

PEOPLE BORN WITH PLUTO IN LEO IN THE SEVENTH HOUSE

1. Lance Rentzel, football player:[5] October 14, 1943, 3:15 p.m. EWT, Flushing, New York.
2. Billie Jean King, tennis champion:[6] November 22, 1943, 11:45 a.m. PWT, Long Beach, California.
3. Henry Winkler, TV star:[6] October 30, 1945, 12:51 p.m. EST, New York, New York.
4. Susan Atkins, Manson follower, criminal:[6] May 7, 1948, 11:21 p.m. PST, San Gabriel, California.

PLUTO IN LEO IN THE EIGHTH HOUSE

Here Pluto is in its natural house; be assured that it will have its own way. These natives crash headlong into grappling with their own will. All eighth house matters constitute the objectives of a battle between the Leo exploitation of ego and the Plutonian forces of death and renewal, combined with the Scorpio desire for honesty and fairness. In this potent placement, the native can be certain that regeneration will take place. It is a natural event; it is only a matter of time.

Joint resources should be handled in an orderly and ethical manner. If these individuals run into trouble in some financial dealings, they might ask themselves, "Am I taking too much? Am I sharing everything with my partner?" If they are not, the situation will backfire causing them to wrestle with their conscience.

In a divorce the Leo craving for the best of everything will fight it out with the equally strong inclination to be generous, almost magnanimous at times. What will the outcome be? Pluto's deep urges can effect the triumph of generosity over selfishness.

In the matter of taxes, the accumulation of Leo trappings eventually comes up for assessment. If they fret about the size of the tax bill it is because the best of everything must sooner or later be paid for and they need to be reminded that like death, taxes are inevitable. The king has to pay them along with the peasants.

With Scorpio on the cusp of the eleventh they understand that friends are a vital part of their life, and in their Leo way these friends are considered a joint resource along with the partner. "My friends are the greatest," they will say with pride. "I give them my loyalty, but in return I demand loyalty from them."

Sometime in life they will feel the compulsion to search the unknown, the metaphysical and occult world, and to understand the depths within themselves. Here these potent and mysterious forces may be easily unlocked as they lie just underneath the surface of the everyday existence. As they research into these studies they may learn about the nature of death and rebirth, the completion of old projects and the starting of new, the purging of self-defeating behavior in the life, and seek an understanding of why they are here. A revitalization will come upon them slowly, but surely. All of these thoughts and energies must be handled with care and channeled into a positive direction. Used negatively, they bring only confusion and unhappiness.

PEOPLE BORN WITH PLUTO IN LEO IN THE EIGHTH HOUSE

1. Hamilton Jordan, White House assistant to President Carter:[9] September 21, 1944, 6:07 p.m. EWT, Charlotte, North Carolina.

2. Goldie Hawn, actress:[11] November 21, 1945, 9:30 a.m. EST, Washington D.C.
3. Arthur Bremmer, criminal:[6] August 31, 1950, 2:40 p.m. CST, Milwaukee, Wisconsin.
4. Linda Lovelace, actress:[3] January 10, 1951, 6:15 a.m. EST, New York, New York.
5. Karen Ann Quinlan, accident victim, in coma:[5] March 29, 1954, 11:43 p.m. EST, Scranton, Pennsylvania.

PLUTO IN LEO IN THE NINTH HOUSE

The Jupiterian-Sagittarian nature of the ninth house may activate these souls to a fundamental concern with morality, education, travel and religious persuasion. They confront the need to discover a philosophy that is realistically in tune with life, and while they may sift through the credos and tenets of many churches they are eventually faced with the innate desire to go deeper and uncover the truth for themselves. Scorpio wants to investigate, explode the myths and bring it all out in the open.

If they are drawn to religious work within the church structure, they must at some time test the basics of what they teach and decide for themselves if they are practical. The doctrine they select must be one they can live with on a daily basis.

On the positive side they can become religious leaders of the highest order attracting multitudes by the grace of their dramatic presence and the projection of love and warmth to all. Carried to extremes they could turn into religious fanatics, using Leo charm to spread unusual precepts, churning up the populace and merging into a demigod for the masses to worship. History is filled with such individuals who came to ignoble ends.

The greatest danger with this placement lies in the frustration activated by the Leo-Scorpio square. These natives expect to be successful in their chosen field and if they should fail, they may hide behind the twelfth house veil of illusion. For a time they may escape into alcohol or drugs, finding a release as they shed their problems and float away on a pink cloud. But escapism has never solved anything and the twelfth house retreat obscures the problem to such an extent that they may not know what it really is. An internal battle rages as Pluto compels them to find their true self by searching through the far reaches of the mind. They may say to themselves, "Why do I say this? Why do I do this? What are my real reasons?" They must find a philosophy and a way of life that is comfortably theirs. If they do not remove the rose-colored glasses and return from the fantasy trip to face reality, they may risk being lost forever in the Neptunian wilderness.

These individuals may be attracted to teaching on the college and university levels. They have all the assets to become inspirational leaders if they so wish. They also would find natural expression in a publishing career. Medical journals, books on sports or possibly macabre and bizarre tales of the unknown would appeal to them. Traveling on a world-wide scale in the import-export business may be another distinct and satisfying avenue. They could gain much experience from travel and it may be that in due time they would accept the eastern or oriental philosophies as their own.

So long as they bring their Scorpio selves out of the twelfth house bondage and utilize positively the great forces of education and true religious feeling at their command, they will emerge as fine human beings.

PEOPLE BORN WITH PLUTO IN LEO IN THE NINTH HOUSE

1. Jose Feliciano, singer:[6] September 10, 1945, 10:00 a.m. EST, Lares, Puerto Rico.
2. Peggy Fleming, skating champion:[13] July 27, 1948, 3:00 p.m. DST, San Jose, California.
3. Margaret Trudeau, wife of Canadian Premier:[5] September 10, 1948, 1:00 p.m., Vancouver, British Columbia.
4. Vida Blue, baseball player:[13] July 28, 1949, 2:10 p.m. CST, Mansfield, Louisiana.
5. Chris Evert, tennis champion:[2] December 21, 1954, 4:30 a.m. EST, Fort Lauderdale, Florida.

PLUTO IN LEO IN THE TENTH HOUSE

In the Capricorn-Saturn angular tenth house, the thunderbolt of the Zodiac zooms to the top. The intensity and drive emanating from these natives pulsate outward like the rhythmic crashes of a drum.

Here the achiever truly achieves. Their worldly ambition ruthlessly pushes them along, sweeping obstacles from their path, expecting obedience and admiration from all. Scorpio on the ascendent reinforces the power-play backlashing from the tenth. By their own authority, they proclaim themselves king, admiring their pedigree and silver spoon, banging loudly on their gold cup to attract attention. If the homage is not forthcoming, the native wastes no time in annihilating the nonbelievers. "Off with their heads!" they shout.

In this situation, the temptation to unleash all the negative forces is strong indeed. Power does not guarantee respect, which Leo tries to wrest from the world, and the conflict springs from the abuse of such abundant power and persuasion. Royal figures are often reduced to lonely monarchs sulking in their corporate headquarters, wondering why the common herd does not love them for themselves. Leos need the reinforcement of love to survive; but they must learn that they cannot demand love. It must be freely given, earned with kindness and consideration, a sympathy for the human condition of those who live and breathe and touch their lives.

Only when Pluto has expelled these negative and selfish motives from the inner self do these people grow in stature and understanding of their fellow beings. Their regeneration will come about with the combined influences of the tenth and the first houses so that through business and professional status they will achieve on a personal basis, channeling their amazing energies in the proper way to inspire leadership for others. Then they will indeed have character that is worthy of respect.

Leos have a great deal in their favor with this position, for they possess a strong self-will, fine organizing abilities, boundless energy, a painstaking diligence, and a kind of overpowering inbred desire to shout from the mountaintops. Only through a deep knowledge of self can they emerge from the subtle traps of the tenth to share their bountiful nature with the rest of the world.

The female of the species, even though she may not pursue a career, can be equally powerful in her way from her fortress in the home. She will rule her domain with an iron hand, wearing the pants and exuding authority. She is anything but helpless. As she controls her environment some of this dynamic energy may flow outward into community, school, church or political activities in a most desirable use of her talents.

PEOPLE BORN WITH PLUTO IN LEO IN THE TENTH HOUSE

1. John Lennon, singer, composer, one of the Beatles:[3] October 9, 1940, 7:00 a.m. GWT, Liverpool, England.
2. Arthur Ashe, tennis champion:[13] July 10, 1943, 1:55 p.m. EWT, Richmond, Virginia.

3. Uri Geller, psychic:[6] December 20, 1946, 2:00 a.m. EET, Tel Aviv, Israel.
4. Sally Struthers, TV actress:[3] July 28, 1947, 10:30 a.m. PST, Portland, Oregon.
5. Princess Anne of England, British Royal Family:[12] August 15, 1950, 10:50 a.m. GMT, London, England.

PLUTO IN LEO IN THE ELEVENTH HOUSE

In the last air sign house, the four elements once again fall into place and are put to work in the struggle for regeneration. Scorpio invades Taurus' earth house, while watery Pluto in fiery Leo, inhabits Aquarius' home base. Fixity reigns. With feet firmly rooted to the ground, these natives labor mightily to discover their true values in the house of brotherly love. They wrestle inwardly to find the comfortable neutral ground between the Leo monarchy and the Aquarian democracy. Here the Pluto power misused could reach awesome and frightening heights in one who could incite mass rioting through mass hypnotism and control over mobs by the sheer impact of personality. Until they learn to change their posture, move their feet and take some steps forward, all their sweating and straining will be in vain. Leo must learn that Pluto's water can be poured into Taurus' earth to bring forth the flowers of humankind, which will then blossom in the warmth of the sun and the pure air of Aquarian love.

Leos' value of themselves comes into conflict with the need to regenerate relationships on a universal level. They expect and demand attention. They want to stand out from the mob. Since they are always conscious of their appearance they often find temporary release from torment by ornamenting themselves with beautiful clothes. It is their safety valve when the world pushes in too much. Along the way the Aquarian teacher assigns the lesson to learn; that they must become aware of the whole of humanity with its inborn rights of equality and self-expression before they themselves can become healthy, functioning individuals. For Leos, writhing and kicking in their straightjackets, it is a difficult lesson to learn. Only when the Plutonian experience shakes them to the core and causes them to depreciate themselves and reassess their values, will they emerge as the strong and vital leaders that they are capable of being. Using the second house influence of Scorpio positively they can gain insight into the shattering problems of the rest of the world and turn their abilities into fund-raising for philanthropic and humanitarian causes. Thus, can they effectuate their need for attention in a highly commendable and worthwhile manner and one of their finest traits, that of generosity, will flow like a river of gold.

PEOPLE BORN WITH PLUTO IN LEO IN THE ELEVENTH HOUSE

1. Cornelia Wallace, wife of Governor George Wallace:[5] January 28, 1939, 9:00 p.m. CST, Elba, Alabama.
2. Richard Speck, mass murderer:[3] December 6, 1941, 1:00 a.m. CST, Kirkwood, Illinois.
3. Freddie Prinz, TV actor:[5] June 22, 1954, 12:58 p.m. EDT, New York, New York.
4. Joe Frazier, boxing champion:[13] January 17, 1944, 9:30 p.m. EST, Beaufort, South Carolina.

PLUTO IN LEO IN THE TWELFTH HOUSE

In the mysterious Neptunian twelfth house, these natives stumble into the compulsion to communicate their thoughts as the square from the Scorpio-Gemini third house activates its energy. The means to express themselves somehow disappears into an ephemeral haze. They experience discomfort and cannot quite put their finger on the cause of it.

Verbal facility does not come easily to people with this placement. At an early age they may encounter difficulty voicing ideas and responses to others, and, feeling uncomfortable, retreat into sullen silences. Trivial chit-chat with family and friends does not appeal to them, partially due to a fear of being misunderstood. If they cannot say something important they prefer to say nothing at all. Leos want to be in the limelight, but in the twelfth house there is fog. How can they be comfortable in the center of the stage when they feel unable to express themselves properly, especially when there is no stage? The native crashes headlong into the invisible twelfth house wall.

When the anxiety of the square is operating at full strength, these individuals can be guilty of harsh speech and cutting words. Their ideas are fixed, stated with authority and firm conviction. If others attempt to present their opinions or disagree with these pronouncements they lash out at them with biting sarcasm. When, inevitably, friends and acquaintances are repulsed by these actions and move away in droves, Leos may curl up in a sullen heap as they try to discover the cause of their unhappiness. The third house influence must backtrack to the twelfth and, with Scorpionic penetration, lift the veil of confusion, sweep aside the mists and stare Pluto in the face.

Until they undergo the Pluto purging their methods of communicating will be their self-undoing. Their pride may be so fierce that it blocks emotions, tying them up into knots. They may be unable to cry for joy, sorrow or rage. All the frustration may reverberate into relationships with loved ones, causing untold havoc.

Sooner or later, under Pluto's tutelage, they will

find the way to release their creative self from the twelfth house bondage of the unconscious mind. By using their Piscean antenna they can tune in to others' thoughts and know their joys and sufferings as their own, understanding from their generous hearts that all humanity shares the common bonds of pleasure and pain. Only then will the self-inflicted communication barriers be knocked down forever. Perhaps by placing their Leo feet in the humble Piscean shoes they will then be able to truly say, "I walk with you, my friends, not on you."

In this position their relationships with brothers and sisters will be deep and intense, marked with Leo loyalty. They may have problems with them at various times but they will always be a vital part of their life.

PEOPLE BORN WITH PLUTO IN LEO IN THE TWELFTH HOUSE

1. Anita Bryant, singer, political activist: March 25, 1940, 3:10 p.m., Barnsdale, Oklahoma.[5]
2. Bob Dylan, singer, composer:[3] May 24, 1941, 9:55 a.m. CST, Duluth, Minnesota.
3. Muhammad Ali, champion boxer:[3] January 18, 1942, 6:30 p.m. CST, Louisville, Kentucky.
4. O. J. Simpson, football player:[6] July 9, 1947, 8:10 a.m. PST, San Francisco, California.
5. Patricia Hearst, heiress, criminal:[3] February 20, 1954, 6:01 p.m. PST, San Francisco, California.

CHAPTER THREE
PLUTO IN VIRGO

TO PLUTO IN VIRGO
WORK

Let me but do my work from day to day,
In field or forest, at the desk or loom,
In roaring market-place or tranquil room;
Let me but find it in my heart to say,
When vagrant wishes beckon me astray,
"This is my work; my blessing, not my doom;
Of all who live, I am the one by whom
This work can best be done in the right way."

–Henry Van Dyke

THE GENERATIONAL CHANGES

October 19, 1956 to January 16, 1957; August 18, 1957 to October 4, 1971; April 17, 1972 to July 30, 1972

In 1956, Pluto left its last mark on the vital Leo generation and spinning along on its eccentric orbit, slid into a comfortable eighteen year sextile with its home base. This marked the period when unflappable Virgo, carrying her harvest basket of dried herbs and wheat germ, smiled demurely at sexy, magnetic Scorpio, and ducking her head modestly, allowed his master Pluto to take over her house and hang out his sign. Water flowed into mutable, fruitful earth and brought forth positive growth in many areas of health, work, and service.

Since the children born during this time span are not yet full-blown adults, we can only speculate on how these Plutonian energies will eventually shape and alter their future. We know only that this generation will be different from the Cancer and Leo ones, carrying a different banner and crusading for other causes in their quietly effective, diligent Virgo way.

Therefore, since we are yet to witness the lasting results of the natal placements, we will discuss here the innumerable changes that occurred in all our lives during the eighteen year transit. Mercury, the ruler of Virgo and broadcaster of news, becomes an important focal point of the spectrum. Its influence permeated the period, since it was, in a sense, a re-styling of our everyday affairs: what we wore to work, what we ate for lunch, how we felt about our bodies and our health. Virgo's message got through to all of us: Clean up the air, clean out the water, clean out your bodies, clean up the world!

The first clean-up, centering on our eating habits, combined Pluto's detective work with Virgo's ability to analyze. By degrees we were confronted with the information that our daily food was far from being pure and wholesome. Untold amounts of adulterants, additives and preservatives had been pumped into thousands of items on the grocery shelves. Cattle and poultry, it was discovered, were shot full of hormones to increase their growth rapidly. Vegetables and fruits were sprayed with controversial insecticides, picked before maturity and ripened artificially. Junk foods, full of empty calories and artifical ingredients, proliferated in the supermarkets and dispensing machines. We were surrounded by tons of food, neatly packaged, highly priced and nutritionally worthless.

Laboratory-produced products, created by chemicals and denatured ingredients, appeared in the stores, presumably to replace real eggs, orange juice, coffee cream and whipping cream, sugar and salt. When the manufacturers were confronted with a list of their perfidious practices, they counterattacked by stating that such methods were necessary in today's mass production and long-range transportation and claiming that overall the materials suspected were not harmful in small doses.

Such flagrant disregard for the national health brought about many consumer advocates, most notably Ralph Nader, who organized movements to guard and protect the consumer from the perils of the market-place and to instigate stricter laws in raising and packaging food. The movement gained momentum as average individuals realized how it all affected them personally, and today, citizen action groups and consumer reports are widespread on television and in magazines and newspapers. The Pluto parallel here is incontestable: the mighty planet uncovered the misuses of our great resources and with the help of Virgo analysis brought it into public view where it could not be ignored. The attack has by no means ceased, but it can be safely noted that Pluto will ultimately win the battle to clean up the food.

As this was occurring, many thoughtful individuals turned to natural foods in silent revolt against devitalized foods. The healthy living crusade was born and in a sincere attempt to stay well, millions of people planted vegetable gardens, baked their own bread, sprouted seeds in glass jars, embraced yogurt and soy beans, drank carrot juice daily and tossed away the white sugar. Thousands of health books tumbled off the presses; vegetarianism, juice fasting and cleansing diets leaped into vogue. The lowly vitamin pill turned into a symbol of a better way of life as people boned up on information concerning the benefits of its well-known alphabet from A through K.

Hand in hand with this movement, the uses of

herbal tonics were explored and, to fill the sudden demand, many herb stores opened up. Strange exotic substances were stocked in row after row of apothecary jars. In rebellion against the high cost of medical care many people experimented with these brews for the relief of simple problems—colds, sore throats, sinus, swellings, bruises, indigestion, sleeplessness—and found that they were often remarkably successful. Herbology became another new subject worthy of study and those who investigated its lore discovered that, in many instances, they were reverting to their great-grandmother's simple home remedies and the centuries-old mixtures passed along by our native Indian tribes. Here again, Pluto was at work excavating something of Virgo value which had long been buried and forgotten.

In this period, obesity was chalked up as America's number one health problem. Statistics indicated that one person out of four was overweight, brought about by the nutritional disasters which masqueraded as meals in many homes; meals heavy with animal fats, white sugar, salt and carbohydrates and singularly lacking in fresh vegetables, fruits and whole grains. Around the same time, fast food chains mushroomed over the country offering food laden with calories and deficient in vitamins and minerals. The public consumed it all in alarming amounts.

In a Virgo counter-attack to the constantly increasing number of double chins and bulging abdomens, fad diets blazed their way into the

American conscience. Every week a different diet flashed from the newsstands: all protein, all carbohydrates, all fat, followed by ones advocating no protein, no carbohydrates, no fat. You could take your pick, and the public usually did. Advice on how to lose the flab flowed like hot fudge sauce from an overturned jug. All this misery needed company, so Weight Watchers and similar supportive groups flourished, augmented by weight reduction clinics and health and exercise clubs. Over-the-counter weight loss pills sold as fast as candy. Any two people meeting casually at a social gathering or on a street corner, sooner or later conversationally brushed up against the latest method of attacking the bulges in an endless quest for the miracle method.

Those who despaired of ever losing the poundage turned to a startling last-ditch Scorpionic method: surgical removal of part of the intestines. Another equally uncomfortable means was total fasting under a doctor's care, drinking water only and taking vitamin supplements. This could be described as the extremes; Virgo's cleansing and Pluto's elimination meeting and joining forces on the medical battlefield.

However, a great many worthwhile results emerged from the Virgoan preoccupation with the physical body. People who previously found it a chore to carry the trash out to the curb now started exercising daily. Riding a bike or walking to work increased in popularity. Yoga, tennis, swimming, golfing, and jumping rope all commanded an army of enthusiasts. But the best method, which subsequently became the most popular, was jogging. From the early morning sprinters to the after-dinner runners, joggers are a common sight in every neighborhood as they toil relentlessly up hill and down dale and around the block once more.

During this period medical doctors found themselves clinging precariously to their pedestals as millions became disenchanted with their perfunctory care. Once considered infallible and an object of respect and devotion they were now often regarded skeptically as capable of making serious errors in judgment. Usually they treated the symptom, not the cause. The mighty drug culture had infiltrated our society and many physicians freely prescribed pills as the cure-all for whatever grave physical or emotional problems were gnawing away at our lives. Surgery was performed in many instances when it was not necessary. The traditional family doctor who was instantly available, understanding and mindful of our pocketbooks, had disappeared from the scene.

However, on the other end of the spectrum, tremendous strides were made in many fields of research, most notably those concerned with mental health, cancer, heart problems and diseases involving debilitating physical handicaps. Many of these subjects had never been openly discussed and those suffering from them had been shunted into the background. Now no disease or medical problem was too delicate or rare to be examined in the mass media. Women who had been victims of breast cancer talked candidly about their rehabilitation. Men with vasectomies commented frankly on the joy of their sex lives. Pluto brought it all up from the depths to be treated with Scorpio honesty and Virgo specialization.

Sex not only came out of the closet, it jumped up and down, turned cartwheels and paraded in public view. Once Pluto-in-Scorpio had gotten the message through to Virgo that sex was a pleasure, not a duty, Virgo accepted the information and added her analytical, detailed touch to it. Tons of material—charts, diagrams, pictures, texts—fell like an avalanche upon the public. Sex was discussed with shattering frankness on television and radio; it was acted out in movies and on the stage, written about in minute detail in books and magazines and graphically illustrated with on-the-spot photographs. In grade school classrooms, sex education was taught in such a forthright manner that the myths of the birds, bees, and long-legged stork vanished forever in the mists of time. No facet of sexuality was too shocking for serious examination—nymphomania, bisexuality, trans-sexuality, impotence, frigidity, homo-sexuality, venereal disease, teenage pregnancies, rape, incest—and the public, reeling under the impact, managed to keep a toehold on common sense and absorbed it all. Pluto broke down the centuries-old barriers of false modesty and hypocrisy to inform us through the comfortable

Virgo sextile that our basic sexual drives were not something to be snickered at, or shamefully hidden, but merely a normal healthy function of the human body.

One of the most widespread and visible changes of the Pluto in Virgo years came about in wearing apparel and personal adornment, as the average young citizen took on the garb of the average worker. From some untracked source, blue jeans shot on to the fashion scene. Everybody, with the possible exception of a few fastidious Virgos, wore them. Their popularity was guaranteed by their beat-up comfort, durability and relatively low cost. Wearing them required allegiance to rule number one: the garment must never, under any circumstances, look new. In order to achieve this desirable end, the levis were stained, patched, and sloshed around in bleach to fade the color to its necessary drabness. Often the trouser legs were hacked off with blunt scissors to acquire the badly-frayed-edge look. It was observed that owners frequently jumped for joy when a pair sprang genuine holes in the knees. Rule number two demanded that they should fit skin tight, just short of stopping the circulation in the thighs. The ultra-rich had theirs custom tailored. High-salaried entertainers studded theirs with rhinestones. They were worn to parties, funerals, weddings, graduations, court rooms, restaurants, appearances before the I.R.S., night clubs and, inescapably, work.

The most fitting accompaniments to all this rampant informality were rumpled and faded blouses, unironed shirts, football jerseys and printed T-shirts which clearly stated one's philosophical outlook on life. If it was necessary, because of the weather, to wear shoes, then sneakers, torn and dirty, were the perfect complement. Otherwise, going barefoot was considered quite smart. From the upper reaches of the mysterious world of fashion fads, the head peanut had proclaimed to all, "Look poor, dammit!" Only by copying the appearance of an unemployed migrant farm worker was one truly "with it."

In keeping with this ungroomed look, the young, as if in response to another ultimatum issued from on high, decided to let their hair grow. And grow it did, anywhere from shoulder length to below the waist on both sexes. On the men, beards and moustaches sprouted, blossomed and bloomed. Hair was everywhere, rippling in the wind, floating in the soup, getting caught in machinery and revolving doors. Young women raised a languid hand and pushed it out of their eyes approximately five hundred times a day. Shampoo manufacturers rallied to the upsurge in consumption of their product as the code demanded that each hairy person wash it, if not constantly, then at least once a day.

Spurred on by the overall informality young women, reacting to a subtle Scorpio compulsion, abandoned bras, panty-house, socks, makeup and good grooming, but held on obstinately to their standard gear—a battered shoulder bag containing ten pounds of miscellaneous equipment. Their male counterparts abandoned underwear (it was rumored), shirts, socks and shoes, thus arriving at the ultimate: blue jeans and nothing more. In an original attempt to find their own individuality and break away from the examples of their elders, they had succeeded in looking totally colorless and totally alike. Perhaps when these young people feel the thrust of Pluto in Libra with the Venusian love of beautiful things, they will change their ways and take pride in their appearance. For here is a whole generation that has never experienced the fun of dressing up and looking their best.

During this same period older women also went through a revolution in clothing. Sometime in the mid-Sixties a lone designer innocently paired women's slacks with coordinated jackets and let loose upon the world the polyester pant suit. It was an overnight sensation and women of all ages, in all walks of life snapped them up, wore then for most occasions and gloried in their easy going comfort after years of too short, too long, too tight or too wide skirts. All subsequent efforts of the New York and Paris fashion elite to shake her out of them and pour her back into dresses have met with considerable resistance.

On the beach, the Virgo interest in clothing and healthy living and the Scorpio desire to undress the body met, tangled briefly and compromised with the bikini. Another Scorpionic style bubbled up from the depths in the miniskirt, whose popularity lasted for several years, meanwhile ruffling up the average male spectator.

In counterbalance to the bare look, saris, mumus and caftans arrived on the scene. Made from splashy prints they were shapeless, all-encompassing garments which heavy women enjoyed wearing. Underneath these garments they didn't have to wear much, either.

The do-it-yourself movement entrenched itself firmly in our daily lives during this transit. Virgo service merged into serve-yourself. All manner of establishments—drug, grocery, gas stations, department stores—informed the public to wait on themselves and pay as they left. In many restaurants customers were their own waiters. Men and women were encouraged to fix a plethora of household gadgets with do-it-yourself advice. Old-fashioned service, geared to individual tastes had practically disappeared from the mainstream of American life.

The Pluto life-and-death influence and the Virgo desire for perfect health expressed itself in various ways, but none with more lasting impact than the merging together of these two forces in the return to natural childbirth. Many expectant mothers decided to embrace the practice, partly in revolt against the high cost of medical care and the assembly line procedures of many hospitals, and partly in a sincere desire to produce a child under normal conditions, as nature had meant it to be. The usual method of being drugged into insensibility during labor was considered and rejected. These young women went through rigorous training in preparation for the birth and, when their time came, found it a deeply meaningful experience which they shared emotionally with their husbands who often were present in the delivery room. These young mothers also chose to breast feed their children and so returned full circle to the natural function of a woman's body.

In the intense concern over ecology and the quality of human life, population control surged forward in importance. Contraceptive information from reliable sources became more readily accessible to any person who sought it. Education on family planning was widely disseminated, particularly among low income groups where it was badly needed.

In the late Fifties, the oral birth control pill was made available after years of research. Millions of women enthusiastically used this method because of its convenience. Inevitably, its use spread to teenagers who, with the relaxation of moral standards, were becoming sexually active in their early teens.

The advocates of abortion, which had been the back-street child of the medical profession for centuries, triumphed over the forces of bigotry and ignorance and abortion became legal, safe and available to any woman who, for social, economic, health or emotional reasons, chose not to bear a child. Slowly but surely the quality of human life was being altered from quantity to quality.

Virgo's love of animals was affected in two ways during the transit. Indiscriminate breeding of cats and dogs had resulted in thousands of unwanted animals who were eventually put to death by the proper authorities. In an effort to eliminate this unhappy and unpleasant situation, campaigns for the neutering of pets were intensified. At the other end of the scale in an effort to save many rare animals from extinction, concerned groups encouraged their protection and the reproduction of their species.

During this period the right-to-die became a vital issue which inevitably concerned every citizen. Could the terminally ill individual choose to die naturally by foregoing the impressive artillery the medical profession could command to keep him breathing a few more weeks or months? Scorpio honesty stripped away the guilt and hypocrisy from these situations and made us face them squarely. Pluto in Virgo demanded that the human body be allowed to die in its own natural way.

During this transit the labor unions strengthened their position in American industry. They sought better and safer working conditions, improved health insurance, shorter working hours and an equal wage scale for men and women, all Virgo concerns. Many groups who had never been on strike before decided to dramatize their grievances. Teachers, hospital employees, policemen, doctors, nurses, bus drivers, taxi drivers and sanitation department employees were among those who not only stopped working and inconvenienced the general public, but in some cases caused genuine hardships. It was their way of saying their work was important and they demanded to be paid well for their contribution to the general welfare.

Looking back over this period we can see the far reaching changes which have taken place. All of these trends have been basically for our own improved health and state of mind—a Scorpio kind of honesty about our daily lives—thinking about what is good for us and what is not. Pluto has pointed directly toward filth and issued its ultimatum: clean it up and live, or let it go and die. Since these movements have occurred peacefully and without rancor, we have a feeling of optimism that Pluto has done its job well, in disposing of the waste and debris and showing us with Virgo precision and organization how we can best improve the qualities of our lives.

PLUTO AND URANUS CONJUNCT IN VIRGO

Uranus in Virgo: November 2, 1961 to January 10, 1962; August 10, 1962 to September 28, 1968; May 22, 1969 to June 24, 1969: Exact Conjunction of Uranus and Pluto from August 29, 1965 to August 15, 1966

The Uranus-Pluto conjunction in the 1960s marked the first occasion of the joining together in the heavens of any two of the three heavy planets since Pluto was discovered in 1930.

The tremendous power of the Aquarian Uranus and the Scorpio Pluto merged together to roll alongside each other and send their vital energies out to stamp the children born under its sway.

Here Pluto, which acts slowly over a long period of time, blends with Uranus which acts suddenly without warning. We catch our breath at the wonderment of it all for never before in recorded history has there been a generation with this particular merging of overwhelming force. What will they do with it? How will it manifest?

Since it occurs in Virgo, the sign of everyday work, health, and service to and from others, its impact will be felt keenly in our lives. As this generation is educated, matures and takes hold of its place in the mainstream of life we can expect to witness the results of its power. All we can be sure of at this time is that great changes will take place in our daily lives; there will be a throwing out of what no longer works or has value and acceptance, and an ushering in of that which is new, startling, revolutionary.

We will watch, our hearts filled with hope and promise, as this generation marches relentlessly forward to a new, a better, a cleaner, a totally revitalized world as the gate to the Age of Aquarius swings open.

PLUTO IN VIRGO THROUGH THE HOUSES

In an effort to help the reader apply the Pluto interpretations presented in this book, we are listing the degrees of importance that Pluto in Virgo assumes when found in the following situations:

1. Pluto is most powerful when the natal Sun is in Scorpio or when there is a stellium in Scorpio.

2. Pluto is powerful when it is in Virgo's natural sixth house or in its own natural eighth house.

3. The power of Pluto is intensified if it is conjunct Mercury.

4. If Pluto is square Mercury in Sagittarius, communication difficulties will be felt strongly. If Pluto is square Mercury in Gemini, the tension is softened somewhat because of Mercury's dual rulership of Gemini and Virgo.

5. If Pluto opposes Mercury in Pisces, a see-saw effect involving one's ability to communicate and function well in the areas of service must be resolved and the forces joined together in a compromise.

6. If Pluto is trine Mercury in Taurus or Capricorn, the ability to communicate will be easily expressed.

7. If Pluto is sextile Mercury in Cancer or Scorpio, an opportunity for growth is present in the houses governed by these signs. Also, a mutual reception exists with Mercury in Scorpio.

8. If Pluto is quincunx Mercury in Aries or Aquarius, tension and strain result because the two planets are not in harmonious elements and are uncomfortable with each other. Often a health aspect is involved.

9. If Pluto is semisextile Mercury in Leo or Libra no special interplay occurs. It is a neutral aspect.

PLUTO IN VIRGO

In the following delineations of house placements, the four elements exist in every other house. Virgo earth in a fire sign house, such as Aries' first house, places Scorpio water in Gemini's natural third air house. When Virgo earth falls in Gemini's natural house Scorpio water is situated in Leo's natural fifth fire house. Thus, in delineating the first, third, fifth, seventh, ninth and eleventh houses, all four elements work in harmony and the sextile opportunity functions with ease.

PLUTO IN VIRGO IN THE FIRST HOUSE

Since the first house is concerned with self and the physical body, the Virgo forces concentrate on matters of health and well-being. These natives will experience the need to keep in shape, to follow sensible diets and to present themselves to the world in the best possible way. This often takes the form of concern over one's wardrobe, a consuming interest in the latest fashions, and the urge to appear immaculately groomed and impeccably clad at all times. Along with the search for perfection, these natives follow the innate need to organize their daily living, to eliminate extraneous matters and to focus their attention on getting things done with order and precision.

Their interest in ecology is personal and carries

over into everyday affairs. They are the individuals who cut down on energy use, drive small cars, and turn in newspapers and cans to be recycled. They often urge others to do the same. They are acutely aware of the fact that their generation is growing up in a world already heavily polluted by the carelessness and wanton waste of previous generations.

With Scorpio on the third, their renewal will come about from learning to communicate well, to express their thoughts in a concise Virgo manner implemented by Scorpio intensity and sincerity. Since it is a sextile aspect with all four elements present this ability emerges with no special strain. They must overcome any tendency to criticize their brothers and sisters in a nagging manner. When they learn that their standards are not necessarily everyone else's, they can then allow others room to grow and develop into their own personalities.

Pluto in the first house adds great strength of character to the individual. Thus, the Virgo person is quietly powerful, but here the strength is not as apparent as it is with the Cancer or Leo placements.

PLUTO IN VIRGO IN THE SECOND HOUSE

Because Virgos are basically shy and timid, their sense of self-worth can be weak. They grow up expecting the world to be neatly categorized into right or wrong, proper or improper, black or white. As they mature they inevitably discover that life is mostly shades of grey and that the guidelines are none too clear. Anticipating perfection from themselves and others, they run headlong into discontent and frustration when it is not forthcoming. Regeneration is experienced when they finally realize that perfection does not exist and even if it did they would be unable to handle it because they, themselves, are not perfect. They need to build structure into their lives, a structure which is founded on the tolerance of other people's values, allowing them the latitude to move about freely.

Scorpio ruling the fourth stresses parental relationships. These natives carry within them strong fourth house memories of their early years. If these feelings are painful, it is because they feel the parents did not live up to their own high expectations. They must purge such feelings from their mind and accept their parents as they are—shortcomings and all. Then they can go forward to create their own set of values with which they are comfortable, putting behind the disappointments they may have suffered.

With this position these types may manage money so well that this ability alone can become a powerful weapon. They blend the Taurean principle of solid material worth, the Virgoan organization and the Pluto-Scorpio influence to search below the surface and merge them into an unusual grasp and understanding of the financial world. They may excel at handling real estate, construction and land development projects. If computerization is involved, so much the better for Virgos.

They may stumble into a barrier with their frugal, analytical method of handling their own money. If they amass tremendous sums, they will find it difficult to spend it freely and enjoy their earthly possessions. They do not express generosity in the true Jupiterian sense, and if they should give away some of their money to humanitarian organizations they may attempt to keep some strings tied to it.

In order to regenerate their values they must become more sensitive to the needs of others. The obsessiveness of Pluto combined with the Virgo attention to detail could easily get out of hand with the result that whatever they do is overdone, and subsequently curls up and dies from too much concern. It can be compared to the great oak tree which starts from a tiny acorn. Only with proper care can it grow into a mighty force.

PLUTO IN VIRGO IN THE THIRD HOUSE

Here the position of Mercury in the chart is especially important as the two signs it rules, Gemini and Virgo, come together to interact. The Gemini influence tends to skim the surface and scatter its forces, leaving behind a trail of unfinished projects and half-baked ideas. The Virgo influence yearns to pigeonhole everything neatly. With this need for organization and order these natives may squirm quietly inside themselves until they learn to harmonize such conflicting energies into an acceptable pattern, using the Gemini urges to hustle up new ideas and the Virgo abilities to knock it all neatly into place.

The basic problem lies in the need to change their way of communicating, for it is in this area that their uneasiness will be apparent. Before they can claim to be authorities, they must have a thorough knowledge of the subject, or they are not ready to step forth into the fifth house limelight. Pluto prods the native into adhering to the Virgo principles in all forms of communication and overcoming the Gemini tendency to verbosity and superficiality. Once this is mastered they can be powerful speakers, or writers, particularly in the fields of research, computer programming, television and radio programming, journalism, education, health, medicine and detective work; in short, any area involving the seeking out and presentation of facts.

On another level of career they can be excellent teachers if they learn to incorporate some Gemini humor and spontaneity into their methods. Virgos often take themselves too seriously and in so doing often overlook the small joys of daily living and intermingling with fellow human beings, a faculty that the Gemini enjoys to the fullest.

PLUTO IN VIRGO IN THE FOURTH HOUSE

The critical Virgos' need is to regenerate and transform themselves from the roots of their being.

From the tenacious Cancer house they feel memories of the past tugging away at the same time that Pluto activates them to prune their roots so that new growth can burst forth. They must eliminate the negative Cancer qualities of obstinately holding on to those they love, and of trying to manipulate them for selfish purposes. In this case it probably includes thrusting perfectionism upon them.

On a daily basis, these individuals may drive themselves ragged trying to maintain an immaculate house and a tidy exterior. Their battle against cobwebs, germs and junk mail will be unflagging. Here is the original squeaky clean person. A square from Mercury to this placement, however, can result in individuals who do not express these ideals of cleanliness and order and consequently nag at themselves for not achieving this. They must learn to harmonize the Virgo disciplines with the Cancer clutching and clutter.

The potential exists in this position for the waters of Scorpio to filter into pure virginal earth from which the tree of life can grow tall and strong. When the tree is strong, its benefits will be felt in the native's sixth house of health and service where its towering branches will give comfort and strength to those who seek shelter and understanding. The Cancer nurturing qualities can be fused with the Virgo practicality to bring forth from the native a remarkable warmth and caring put to work in a productive way.

PLUTO IN VIRGO IN THE FIFTH HOUSE

These types will be discriminating while at the same time deeply emotional in fifth house matters. They will think to themselves, "When I fall in love it will be forever—and perfect. You will be perfect and I will be perfect." They will anticipate that their love affair will express the ultimate in glamour and romance, patterned after the beautiful people languishing in the perfume and liquor advertisements. They envision themselves garbed in the latest smart clothes accompanied by the beloved, an extraordinarily attractive human being with a perfect body and sex appeal oozing from every pore. They may analyze their emotions endlessly, categorizing their feelings, pigeonholing every reaction, computerizing each embrace and in so doing, grind the whole experience into the ground.

Such rigid demands and expectations will bring a man face to face eventually with reality and the uncomfortable knowledge that the girl of his dreams does not always look her best or even behave in the proper way, that her apartment may be untidy and she may be slouching around with chipped nail polish and curlers in her hair. A woman with this position may be appalled at the sight of her lover turning up late with five o'clock shadow, barefoot in scruffy slacks, yawning and scratching. The love affair, like any of life's skirmishes, is not going to be perfect.

They will naturally expect their children to be well-mannered, well-behaved models of deportment. At least they would like to think so and would strive to pour them into such molds. As the children mature and break away from parental domination it will be necessary to reassess them as individuals in their own right.

When the native realizes that life does not offer up models of perfection and the people are people, warts and all, they will be ready for Pluto to goad them into meaningful changes in close relationships.

PLUTO IN VIRGO IN THE SIXTH HOUSE

In Virgo's own house, preoccupation with one's body reaches its peak. The natives pursue good health in all the accepted ways: diet, exercise and hygiene. Plutonian excesses surface when they become overly concerned with their well-being and develop into hypochondriacs or possibly experience mental problems. They pull up from their subconscious the fear of all bodily functions going wrong with the resultant terrifying possibilities. They must learn to temper this concern with common sense so that they achieve and maintain good health without beating themselves to a pulp.

Scorpio in the eighth is also in its own house and likewise exerts strong pressure. The natives have a consuming interest in all that is hidden within the self, both mental and physical, and may be attracted to psychiatry, psychology and research into other areas of medicine. They understand how the power of the mind can make one sick or cure one of illness. They may pioneer Plutonian methods of digging deep into the psyche in order to affect both mental and physical cures for many maladies now afflicting mankind. They are ardent advocates of preventative medicine.

The polarity of the twelfth house suggests that the natives may respond to Neptunian sensitivity and blend it into their contacts with others, especially if they are physicians or nurses. They figuratively will be able to put themselves in the other person's shoes. This ability would be invaluable in diagnosing ailments and following through with the proper treatment. They also would have strong leanings toward the study and investigation of life-after-death phenomena.

In whatever they undertake, they will be fine, disciplined and dedicated workers, using their analytical and scientific abilities to the utmost. With Pluto here, Virgo loses some of its mutability and takes on Scorpio's fixity so that they stick to the job at hand until it is successfully concluded. Much can be accomplished here with both Virgo and Scorpio in their own earth and water houses, feeding each other in a positive manner.

PLUTO IN VIRGO IN THE SEVENTH HOUSE

In Libra's house, the manner in which these natives handle involvements with others is paramount and will naturally flavor the whole life. These individuals take the state of marriage seriously, expecting intellectual and philosophical accord with their partner. From Scorpio tenanting the ninth, a heavy religious overtone to the relationship may be in evidence. The Virgo person may meet the mate overseas in a foreign country or through the realms of higher education or religion.

The natives' inborn power struggles for dominance over the partner. They themselves do not want nor look for any help, but are often guilty of forcing unwanted advice and opinions upon others. They may control a relationship verbally by always having the last word in an argument. They may force religious or philosophical beliefs on others, giving them practical Virgo facts to back up their premises. They may not allow the spouse any freedom to express personal preferences in the daily bonds of matrimony, but insist on being the dominant one in the household. If these types use their negative traits of nagging and complaining, with their demand for perfection, the marriage will be uncomfortable and unhappy. More unions have broken up on the rocks of criticism, recriminations, and attempts to force the other person into one's ideal image than for any other reason. This compulsion toward domination could be reversed in a relationship, with the Pluto-in-Virgo natives on the receiving end, being forced to endure the ordeal of having the mold of perfection projected onto them by the partner.

Here the Plutonian choice is extremely clear. In order to live in Libran harmony with themselves and others, these natives must overcome the negative pressure toward perfectionism and learn to love and accept each person for his or her uniqueness. Only then will they be able to appreciate and enjoy harmonious relationships.

PLUTO IN VIRGO IN THE EIGHTH HOUSE

Pluto in its own house dramatizes power and here it can be incorporated with the use of other people's money. These natives can be titans in the business world as they manipulate trends on the stock market, insurance, bank loans, investment counseling or international finance. They are entirely at ease pulling the strings of influence and juggling tremendous sums of money to their own advantage. A trine or sextile aspect from Mercury would indicate success and a discordant hard aspect an endless struggle for control.

The Scorpio-Pluto configuration quickens a natural concern for a workable solution to the problem of sludge and filth that humankind has created in the world. Their fine Virgo abilities are capable of inventing practical systems to harness solar heat for daily use, to discover new forms of energy to replace the rapidly diminishing supply of fossil fuels, to develop sensible methods for recycling solid waste and to create efficient ways of removing toxic wastes from water and soil.

It is obvious that the melding of the Virgo-Scorpio skills has the potential for lasting good for the earth if properly focused on the problems besetting us all. Pluto can mean death: the death of all humankind. Virgo hears the screams of the dying planet: "Clean it up or you will die! Clean it up or you will never be reborn!" It is a tremendous challenge indeed, and hopefully from the young people born with this powerful fusing of energies, those with the ambition, fine intelligence, drive and concern to accomplish this work of utmost urgency, will come forth.

PLUTO IN VIRGO IN THE NINTH HOUSE

All four elements come together in this placement giving rise to the possibility of peace for all humankind in Jupiter's house with Scorpio tenanting Aquarius' house—or just the opposite: the ultimate destruction of the planet. The symbol of the atomic bomb let loose upon the world can cause complete destruction with the four elements: raging fires, chaotic earthquakes, poisoned air, and polluted water, unleashed and beyond control. If world-wide power is not disciplined by the highest Sagittarian-Aquarian philosophies and understandings, among all nations, and aided at the same time by the extraordinary Virgoan practical health-conscious energies, we will all be headed for extinction.

This generation will gather up all of the stark,

shocking and inescapable statements about our future, and we must believe and act upon them in order to save ourselves. Also from these ranks will come those who will clear away unrealistic religions and philosophies from our daily lives and give us in their place more workable Aquarian methods of living in harmony with our brothers and sisters.

These natives will be faced with the awesome choice of using their educational and religious powers toward finding a better life for all, or of turning their backs and ignoring the clarion call of humankind.

PLUTO IN VIRGO IN THE TENTH HOUSE

In Saturn's own house Pluto propels one toward splendid accomplishments in career. With the hidden Scorpio-Pisces resources of the twelfth, these individuals may have more going for them than is apparent on the surface. Their power may be subtle, a behind-the-scenes exertion of strength, or they may be psychically tuned in to those around them. Either way, they reach for and usually attain their ambitious goals.

Many areas are open to them if they use the best of the Virgo-Scorpio talents. They would make excellent administrators of large institutions where the need to control and discipline others is essential. Secret government work which would involve tracking down covert operations and ferreting out a maize of details would be a fine choice. The

Neptunian twelfth house influence combined with the Virgo interest in clothes could blossom into accomplishment in the field of fabric and fashion design. The endless details involved in motion picture production and direction coupled with an understanding of financing and money management would also have great appeal.

Once they have faced the hidden parts of the psyche, the unconscious motivations obscured in the twelfth house, and come to terms with their real motives, they can then be vehicles for the positive reservoir of power packed into the first house. Regeneration will be experienced when they acknowledge the fact that power must be cultivated and asserted for the good of all and not for selfish, greedy motives. They have abundant power. How will they use it? The choices will be theirs when they come face to face with Pluto.

PLUTO IN VIRGO IN THE ELEVENTH HOUSE

With the fusion of Virgo in Aquarius' eleventh house and Scorpio in the first, these natives metamorphose into their own best friend. They channel their distinctly personal energies into the activities of humanitarian organizations. They work enthusiastically, tirelessly and often on an unpaid basis for the causes they wholeheartedly support. In this involvement they make many friends, but in intimate alliances they prefer quality, not quantity. Their natural Virgo selectivity works to their advantage as they can choose those for whom they have an innate respect and admiration, and separate those who are involved in these activities for their own selfish ends.

This placement may bring out the original angry young man or woman, obsessed with the state of the world and expressing an intense desire to get rid of its evils—overnight, if possible. These types may have suffered through an unhealthy or debilitating experience, such as exposure to radiation, which compels them to vent their wrath on those who have tampered with the balance of nature. Using dramatic eloquence to draw attention to their crusades, they hurl themselves into working ceaselessly for their cause.

Often these natives feel they have a dynamic blueprint for their lives which must be followed to arrive at their predestined goal. The sextile aspect and the presence of the four elements propel them forward toward their objectives with ease. No obstacles litter the path here if they put the finer Virgo-Scorpio qualities into productive expression. They pursue their aims alone with their own inner resources, expecting no help from anyone along the way. Here is the rugged individual blending the Aries fire, Aquarian air, Virgo earth and Scorpio water to create a lifetime crammed with tremendous achievements.

PLUTO IN VIRGO IN THE TWELFTH HOUSE

The Virgo eagerness to tidy it up or throw it away coalesces here with the hidden forces of the twelfth house unconscious. These natives are brought up short with the need to clean out the closet of the mind and sweep up the cobwebs in the damp and murky basement of the psyche before they can erect an enduring framework based on the Scorpio values blueprinted in the second house.

They can be their own worst enemy, turning others away with their constant criticism. If they place an unrealistic assessment on money and possessions, hoarding instead of sharing openly in productive ways, they may be building their own prison. They must meet the world head on instead of hiding in the twelfth, and project in a positive way, combining the finest Virgo-Scorpio qualities, and balanced by the Libran influences in the first house.

The Virgo analyzation can be invaluable in the desire to know and understand themselves as they confront the computerized details that make up their Pluto-in-Virgo soul. The search will be intense and they will constantly question their beliefs until the Pluto regenerative experience happens. It will take place—of that they can be certain, or Pluto would not be posited in the twelfth house.

Virgo earth and Scorpio water here combine to plant the seeds of a good life, involving honest, hard work in a productive service to others. In this twelfth house position, Pluto rises from the depths, making itself plainly visible as it proclaims to the native and to the world, in one final blast: "The time has come to clean up your act!"

CHAPTER FOUR
PLUTO IN LIBRA

PLUTO IN LIBRA

"Come live with me and be my love–"
–Christopher Marlowe

"Poetic justice, with her lifted scale,
Where, in nice balance, truth with gold
she weighs–"
–Alexander Pope

THE GENERATIONAL CHANGES

October 4, 1971 to April 17, 1972; July 30, 1972 to November 20, 1983; May 20, 1984 to July 29, 1984

In October, 1971, Pluto completed its journey through Virgo's realm and, moving slowly forward in its pathway, entered Libra's house. Uranus transiting through this sign from 1968 to 1974 had disrupted the social order, causing the scales to swing wildly out of balance. Now the time had come for the power planet to stabilize the scales using the Libran intellect and the Scorpionic regeneration to bear upon the areas of justice and equality in our daily concerns. Since seventh and eighth house meanings always involve other persons in our lives, not just our individual selves, Pluto's influence reaches out and entwines us all.

When it was discovered in 1930, Pluto was in the water sign, Cancer. Since then it has traveled through the fire sign, Leo, and the earth sign, Virgo. Presently, the astrological world has the opportunity to catalog its effects in the air sign, Libra, providing us with the chance to observe its merging with the last of the four elements.

Once again, as with the Virgo placement, we can only deliberate on the long-range results of this powerhouse position. The children born under this configuration are far too young to provide astrologers any definite feedback from their life experiences. All we can do is wait and see how the strength of its impact will manifest in them as individuals and as members of this dynamic generation destined for tremendous upheaval in the world.

Thus we will consider the transitions presently taking place or in the process of realization in all our lives as Pluto rolls inevitably forward on its way to its Scorpio home.

With this transit, slowly but surely, the behavioral patterns and ethical standards of marriage are undergoing drastic change. For centuries women had entered into the marriage state for financial security and the chance to bear children in a protected environment while men married to avail themselves of a convenient, morally acceptable outlet for their sexuality, to beget children and to acquire a dependable live-in housekeeper, cook, nursemaid and hostess. The meaning of the words partner, companion and lover were hardly considered and certainly not taken seriously. Men expected their women to be weak and dependent, for in that way they controlled them. Widows and divorcees, jolted out of their comfortable station, searched frantically for another husband to take over their burdens. Likewise, widowers unable to cope with raising children and running a household by themselves rushed to the altar with wife number two as soon as the prescribed period of mourning had passed. This one-hand-washing-the-other routine was a questionable bargain that had endured because society had never critically examined its pattern.

Under the Uranus-in-Libra and Pluto-in-Leo transits young adults originated the life styles of openly living together in a sexual relationship free of any legal entanglements. They were rebelling against the strict moral code of their elders, a code which they had observed first-hand as having fostered emotional disasters, brought about by hypocritical role-playing and unrealistic expectations of lifelong fidelity. These young people embraced the idea that short term casual pairing, a random coming and going arrangement, was vastly preferable to one in which two individuals were bound, supposedly forever, by the rigid conventions of religion and the law.

Relationships were easy to enter into and in many cases where possessions were meager, just as easy to conclude. When disenchantment set in, each person simply packed up his or her clothing, books, records, sleeping bag and musical instrument and, as the jargon of the time put it, "split." However, when older people involved themselves in living in the same place with a welter of his and her furniture, household trappings, personal belongings and objects they had purchased together the rights of ownership became confused if and when they broke up the union. Two unmarried persons buying a house or apartment together discovered many messy legal entanglements. If a child was born to the couple, the situation was even more complicated with the rights of each parent hazy and undefined.

These were merely the practical aspects. The

emotional scars could be lasting and deep from too many casual encounters, a constant searching for sexual excitement and an unwillingness to take any relationship seriously. Even with its drawbacks, though, this living together for awhile gave these young people something their parents had never experienced: the chance to know each other honestly, without pretense or posture, and to communicate openly about their desires and expectations. It is a long way from the Pluto-in-Cancer generation which was steeped in the regimented code of their time—strict morality and romantic nonsense. If this casual living together is to remain an accepted life-style, perhaps in time a flexible, renewable legal contract will be devised which will straddle the issue and bring dignity to the relationship.

On the other side of the coin, divorce has now permeated the fabric of our national life to such an extent that one out of every three marriages ends up in the courts. In years past the divorced woman was considered either an unfortunate individual, something of a social leper, or a hot-blooded siren out to snare other women's husbands and smash up homes. Needless to say, she was not sought after. Now her image has changed. The present-day divorcee is a person in her own right who often is working to support herself and several young children while trying to keep her head above the financial waves. The divorced man always was and still is a highly desirable person from the social standpoint. However, instead of projecting the carefree playboy image of bygone days, he is usually working diligently to pay child support to his ex-wife and the rent on his own apartment. These millions of divorced persons are now accepted matter-of-factly by everyone as part of the pattern of our daily lives.

In many states, divorce has become easily attainable by using such neutral phrases as "irreconcilable differences" and "irretrievable breakdown in the marriage" for the grounds. Gone forever are the times when trumped-up charges of adultery were necessary to provide the only acceptable legal reason, or when the laws necessitated one supposedly innocent party heaping horrendous blame on the other for the failure of the marriage. Pluto has swept aside these outmoded concepts. We have matured sufficiently to accept the fact that when a marriage does not work, it is a private matter between two people and should be concluded with their dignity and self respect intact. No court in the land can rule on anyone's emotions.

The women's liberation movement, starting in the late 1960s, has such vast, far-reaching impact that it would be impossible to cover all the changes it will eventually bring about. Pluto's journey through Libra guarantees that womanhood will be released from the age-old chains of restrictions and will be given equal status and opportunity in every aspect of daily living. No longer second-class citizens, women will be free to utilize their talents for the betterment of all.

The civil rights movement, which flamed into action under the Pluto in Leo generation, is now on a steadier course. Much has been achieved for the rights of all citizens, but much still remains to be done. Some of us are still burdened with prejudice, most notably the Pluto-in-Cancer generation which grew up with the black and white worlds neatly defined and no communication between them. The Leo and Virgo generations have accepted the equality of races as a good, natural and healthy concept, and as they become parents they are instilling in their children a regard for the rights of all regardless of race, color or creed. The Pluto-in-Virgo and Pluto-in-Libra children now growing up witness equality around them everywhere as the races mingle freely in all areas of life: schools, colleges, politics, professions, business, entertainment, government, and the arts. It would probably amaze these young people to be reminded that not too long ago a black person was not allowed to enter a restaurant to be served a meal along with white patrons. We have, indeed, made strides.

The Watergate affair, the greatest political scandal of our history, first broke into the news in 1972 when Uranus was transiting through the latter half of Libra and Pluto was just entering Libra. The entire nation was traumatized, grappling with shock and disillusionment, as Pluto relentlessly uncovered the crimes of persons in high places, eventually bringing them all to the courts of justice. As a result, many sweeping changes, legal and otherwise, were instigated into the political processes so that such blatant misuse of power and other people's resources could not happen again.

Pluto as the ruler of Scorpio and the eighth house has brought to the surface for honest examination our primary feelings and our methods of dealing with death. The medical profession, with its highly sophisticated scientific instruments, is able to keep a suffering human being alive for days, months and, in some cases, years longer than he or she would normally have lived, and often at tremendous cost. In the case of the elderly, hopelessly handicapped, or terminally ill patients such impersonal, artificial support of the body's systems has been questioned from an ethical, religious and moral point of view. Our culture has always been unwilling and somewhat embarrassed to face a discussion of death– its circumstances, its causes, its results. Pluto's tutelage is telling us that death is merely a part of life and should be considered and handled with honesty and candor afforded all phases of existence. It will not go away and it cannot be ignored. We are finally learning to accept it with a greater degree of naturalness and ease along with the Plutonian principle that we have the right to die in the manner that nature intended.

Before Pluto ends its journey through Libra, other vital matters will be measured out as the scales seek to find their own level of justice and understanding. If humankind puts to work all these Plutonian forces that have been unleashed thus far in our lifetimes–the Cancer nurturing, the Leo honesty and strong leadership, the Virgo analyzation and the Libran sense of fair play–then we will be able to solve the centuries' old dilemmas of hunger, poverty, slavery, disease and war. The human race now has the tools to accomplish that which was only dreamed of before.

There is hope for the future. We have lived through the transits of the planet of regeneration, and since we are all still here plodding hopefully and optimistically towards a better tomorrow, then we must indeed be doing something right.

Ahead lies the critical Pluto transit through Scorpio, its own sign, where it wields the greatest power. We do not know what it will bring to the universe, or to each one of us. We know only that we have the opportunity—and the choice is ours—to use its strength for the salvation of humankind or to slide into oblivion in a holocaust of self-destruction.

Which way will we go? Is it the end—or is it the beginning?

PLUTO IN LIBRA THROUGH THE HOUSES

In an effort to help the reader apply the Pluto interpretations presented in this book we are listing the degrees of importance that Pluto in Libra assumes when found in the following situations:

1. Pluto is most powerful when the natal Sun is in Scorpio or when there is a stellium in Scorpio.
2. Pluto is powerful when it is in Libra's natural seventh house or in its own natural eighth house.
3. The power of Pluto is intensified if it is conjunct Venus.

4. If Pluto is square Venus in Cancer or Capricorn, the ability to express love and to function harmoniously in family or society will be hindered.

5. If Pluto opposes Venus in Aries, a seesaw effect centering on the native's ability to express love and receive love will need to be resolved and a compromise affected.

6. If Pluto is trine Venus in Aquarius or Gemini, the ability to express love and to integrate into society will be easily expressed.

7. If Pluto is sextile Venus in Leo or Sagittarius, an opportunity for growth is present in the houses governed by these signs. The love nature will be outgoing and function with ease.

8. If Pluto is quincunx Venus in Pisces or Taurus, tension and strain result because the two planets are not in harmonious elements and are uncomfortable with each other. The Taurus placement is softened somewhat because of Venus' dual rulership of Libra and Taurus. Often a health aspect is involved.

9. If Pluto is semisextile Venus in Virgo or Scorpio no special interplay occurs. However, Venus in Scorpio is in mutual reception with Pluto in Libra adding strength to the placement.

PLUTO IN LIBRA IN THE FIRST HOUSE

The all-time charmer, concealing Plutonian power behind a screen of social graces, steps out here to dazzle the world. The Venusian magnetism asserts itself in the poise and grace the native displays to all.

Their Scorpio values from the second house are right up front and on view. They are not only sure of what they want, but also know how to get it, as they subtly maneuver others into doing their bidding and liking them for it. They are seldom crude or bossy, for they know their sweet smiles and elegant manners will win out for them every time.

PLUTO IN LIBRA IN THE SECOND HOUSE

These natives give in to the urge to collect objects of beauty with which they surround themselves. Their values center on their personal possessions of which they are quite proud.

They communicate to others affably, putting them at their ease. When the occasion arises, they can utter soothing words of understanding and help to those who are distressed. Relationships with neighbors and siblings run along smoothly as they have the talent to approach others in a gracious manner.

PLUTO IN LIBRA IN THE THIRD HOUSE

In the Gemini house, the Libran charm expands into the area of public speaking. These individuals will be most effective and dramatic speakers with resonant voices. An appealing, nurturing quality will be present in their words. They would make excellent counselors as they gain the confidence of others who then find it easy to open up and unload personal problems.

They have the ability to write well in several fields: autobiographical material, interior decorating, cooking and journalism. They have strong interests in family backgrounds and their own beginnings.

PLUTO IN LIBRA IN THE FOURTH HOUSE

Here the fifth house qualities, merging with the fourth, bring about better understanding of one's parents and an absorbing preoccupation with children. These natives create beautiful homes, filled with artistic and creative objects, which are always open to family and friends. They may express feelings through painting, and even though they may not be especially talented, they find this a worthwhile outlet for their emotional energies.

Amateur theatrics or other activities which would give them the chance to perform in front of small gatherings might also be another interest bringing satisfaction and enjoyment.

PLUTO IN LIBRA IN THE FIFTH HOUSE

Here the creative urges focus on keeping the body beautiful and healthy. These individuals will also prod their spouse and children into following strict regimes to stay in good condition.

In their working situation, harmony must prevail or they will eventually suffer miserably from any coarse interaction with co-workers or superiors.

Their love affairs will be handled with delicacy and feeling as they set the stage for romance with candlelight, music and flowers. The Libran types find it imperative to do the correct thing at all times or they experience great discomfort. They wish always to avoid embarrassment for themselves and others.

Their children will be well-behaved, mannerly and given the best they can afford. In this fifth house position, Libras seek the spotlight, but only for the appreciation they think they deserve.

PLUTO IN LIBRA IN THE SIXTH HOUSE

Individuals with this placement will expect equality in marriage as the Scorpio seventh house energies flow into the Libran sixth. An uncomfortable situation will break out if one partner attempts to force the other into a servant's role. Both must realize that the most satisfying and successful marriages are based on mutual sharing.

Also, fine opportunities are shown here for a couple with many similar interests and hobbies to consolidate their enthusiasms into a business of their own.

If health problems crop up, these natives may

show the tendency to jump from one side of the scale to the other by following a strict health regime or wallowing in constant concern over their bodily processes.

These individuals will thrive best in an atmosphere of peace and harmony in their daily lives, especially within their working conditions. In career matters, their Venusian touch may be directed toward dealing in art or other fields of artistic endeavors. They would also be attracted to medicine, psychology, and the counseling professions.

PLUTO IN LIBRA IN THE SEVENTH HOUSE

An excellent opportunity comes along here for the native to use mutual resources and responsibility in forming a partnership. Both the native and the mate are strong individuals and they speak the same language, since Libra is in its own house and fuses easily into Scorpio's own house. Venus and Pluto hold hands in happy companionship and, if properly directed and used, these fine harmonious energies can blend into a beautiful strong marriage and an inspiring business partnership.

PLUTO IN LIBRA IN THE EIGHTH HOUSE

These natives live their daily lives involved with ninth house matters of philosophy and religion.

They must study and work hard to discover their own way and to disregard any disturbing impressions coming from others as they expound on their own philosophies. Much time is needed as they reflect on the mysteries of life before making the final choice on which road they will follow throughout their years. They regenerate themselves through the sincere application of their chosen creed, which they apply not only to themselves but to their partner as well.

If they are involved with others' resources they must discipline themselves always to be fair. Thoughts of life after death intrigue them and they may spend much time in its critical evaluation.

Many careers are open to them: minister, priest, disciple of foreign cultures, teacher, lecturer, philosopher. If too much stress is brought to bear on this placement, the negative forces might swerve them toward fanaticism.

PLUTO IN LIBRA IN THE NINTH HOUSE

Persons who achieve fame, possibly before they are ready to accept its responsibilities, are spotlighted here. Desire for worldly renown consumes them, but Pluto warns that they must find inside themselves the right creed to follow for successful living before they can truly fulfill their destiny. If they apply the finest influences of the ninth house, their accomplishments will be tremendous.

With Aquarius on the ascendent, these natives are concerned with the rights of fellow human beings. This potent placement may lead them toward government and political leadership.

PLUTO IN LIBRA IN THE TENTH HOUSE

The good-will ambassador, the philanthropist, the shrewd business tycoon or the distinguished lawyer can develop from this combination. With Scorpio on Aquarius' eleventh house, joining together Pluto and Uranus, old structures no longer needed will be replaced by new and startling innovations. Here is the native with the power to perform these changes: the trail blazer, stressing equality for all. Perhaps our first woman president will have this placement.

PLUTO IN LIBRA IN THE ELEVENTH HOUSE

From Scorpio in the twelfth house, the hidden power merges with the Libran eleventh house Aquarian traits to bless these natives with stupendous inner strength. They themselves will not be conscious of such powers until some grave crisis erupts in their lives and unleashes the potency of their inner being. Then it will surge forth to aid in reaching their goals. The Sagittarian optimism, shining out from the ascendent, adds to the natives' talents so that these forces can blend to work for the good of humankind.

PLUTO IN LIBRA IN THE TWELFTH HOUSE

Until they explore the twelfth house secrets of the inner-self, these natives can be their own worst enemy. Pluto, from the depths, demands that they penetrate the veil of illusion and learn to adjust to the needs of others. When they realize that no one can live alone all the time, the Libran power of Venus will guide them toward a happier existence where love and harmony are generously given and shared.

CHAPTER FIVE
PLUTO IN SCORPIO

PLUTO IN SCORPIO
1983 TO 1995

"The future has several names. For the weak it is impossible. For the fainthearted it is the unknown. For the thoughtful and valiant it is the ideal. The challenge is urgent, the task is large; the time is now."

—Victor Hugo
1802-1885

THE GENERATIONAL POTENTIALITY

November 20, 1983 to May 20, 1984; July 29, 1984 to January 1, 1995; April 23, 1995 to November 18, 1995

Since its discovery in 1930, Pluto has slowly pushed and wound its eccentric way forward through four highly personal signs: Cancer, Leo, Virgo and Libra. When it enters Scorpio in November, 1983, its long journey homeward will be over. The astrological world has never before had the opportunity to observe this transit, merging the power of the most distant planet with the power of Scorpio. Just as any planet functions with ease in its own sign, so here, Pluto, ruler of Scorpio and the eighth house, is comfortable. In its travels it has flowed into Cancer, battled its way through Leo, prodded Virgo along and merged with the social concepts of Libra. In Scorpio it represents absolute power unparalleled by the strengths and weaknesses of the preceding signs.

Interlocking with Cancer and Pisces in the water trine, Pluto in Scorpio generates the power to feel, to nurture, to express compassion for all of humanity. Cardinal Cancer can be a rushing river or a bubbling stream, fixed Scorpio deep water or ice, while mutable Pisces, its fish swimming in opposite currents, fluidity and the ability to go in whatever direction one chooses. Many choices are available, as many as the ways in which water itself can be changed and used.

What, then, is power? How is this raw energy to be channeled and contained? First, there is the soft spring rain soaking into the ground and feeding the seeds of plants and flowers as they lie in darkness beneath the soil. Then as the seeds reach upward for the sun's warmth, they grow and ripen, and their harvest sustains us through the years. But too much rain pounding on the earth can wash new seeds away or rot the plants and undermine the structures of the buildings in which we live. The gentle snow can also melt into the ground to fertilize the seeds, keeping them protected under its blanket through the long winter months. But too much snow caves in roofs, disintegrates roads and paralyzes commerce. Ice can be used to preserve food, but too much ice wreaks havoc with transportation and endangers ships at sea. The raging river can overflow its banks and sweep the earth before it in a torrent of destruction. But, properly channeled, the water can be contained by a dam which turns its unbridled energy into electricity bringing heat and light, convenience and comfort.

The very nature of water is motion, movement, and its presence is essential for human life. Its fluidity presents us with more options than we had thought possible. So also is the weapon of power around us in many forms, the seen and unseen, accepted or rejected. We are all born with emotions and feelings, a vital part of ourselves, and Pluto represents—as nothing else can—this raw power which lies within. The question is and always will be: how will this emotional power be used? Power can lead and inspire, it can care for and nurture, it can explode and shatter, and it can also become the carpet-bagger of the soul.

So we are brought up short to examine the text book concept of the Scorpio power with its rampant negativity, its emphasis on sex and death, its intolerance and ruthlessness, its withdrawal into self which somehow becomes insidious. We cannot accept such a premise. Since astrology is based largely on the concept of polarity, why then does not Scorpio, opposite the Taurean Venusian second house, represent awareness and acceptance of other people's values? Truly, this basic need for understanding our fellow creatures grows inevitably from the passage through its neighbor, the Libran seventh house, which prepared the native for the utmost that the Scorpio eighth house has to offer. No death is involved here unless it is the death of one's own absorption in self, and the limits of acknowledging only one's own code of behavior.

Here sex is expressed not through the experience of casual, amoral adventures alluding to Scorpio's urges and capacities, but in the passion of two individuals deeply in love and energizing that love in a fusion of souls. For passion in its highest sense is a quality of the soul; without it, sex is meaningless, empty and futile.

From its basis of emotionality, Scorpio reaches across the zodiac to its counterpart, Taurus, and blends its intensity with feelings of self worth, values, and warm, affectionate responses to others.

Scorpio seeks to know how others react to love and friendship, what makes them tick, what gets them through the day. The purpose lies not in compelling them to follow or lead, but in integrating both sets of values into a relationship that works. The individual must learn to adjust to a varying set of principles in order to function as a complete person at peace with one's self and fellow human beings.

Along the way humankind has learned many lessons from Pluto's passage. Now we are ready for the most important one as Pluto strips away the veil of secrecy from its own house and proclaims its rallying cry: preparation for humanity's involvement with all peoples and all nations on a level never experienced before.

We must first come to terms with the knowledge that other countries with their unique cultures, religions and standards are entitled to their beliefs. Who are we to insist that ours are better? If we try to inflict our standards upon them, disruption and chaos on a global scale may result. The true Plutonian law demands that everyone, be they a partner or a nation, should be listened to and appreciated for their individuality, for in trying to limit them, we are in effect limiting ourselves.

Renewal and regeneration must first begin with the individual's own life before spreading outward. Unless one undergoes the joy of this experience, one will suffer a kind of death, a psychological block to the emotions, and will end up powerless, half alive, searching for the justice in life's many burdens. When the eighth house has absorbed the meaning of the second and intertwined it with its own strengths, then the native will indeed understand that compassion, acceptance of one's fellows as they are, and a clear value of one's self are the most prized possessions.

From the Cancerian fourth house of the water trine, the native looks out to see the world in conflict. Only when one has known the eighth house acceptance will he or she be able to travel the high road to the ultimate compassion of Pisces, and reach up from the Stygian depths to the glory and brightness of the stars.

PLUTO IN SCORPIO IN THE FIRST HOUSE

From the first house emerges the penetrating personality, searching passionately for answers to relationships. Deep inside, these natives feel worthless until they find and understand what their own powers and resources are; what they operate with, what their morals and ethics are, and how they can best direct their life. When they uncover this treasure-trove, they will then seek out soul-mates to share their riches.

With Capricorn in the third house putting up its front of role-playing and respectability, they may be frustrated for awhile, finding it hard to bend and meet people on their level. Outsiders may not at first comprehend this yearning for companionship and love, since the native is difficult to know, but with Sagittarius on the cusp of the second house, they persevere for they have much to offer and share.

Optimism and vision radiate from the second house across to the Scorpio natural eighth where Gemini's diversity and liveliness are easily intermingled with the Sagittarian second. Integration of values can bring joy through acceptance and understanding.

PLUTO IN SCORPIO IN THE SECOND HOUSE

The natives' ability to know and assess their true standards and self-worth is helped considerably by Pluto's presence, but tension can result from Scorpio's opposition to its own house. With Taurus in the eighth, the natural placement of the two signs is reversed. Subtle interplay of the basic forces takes place resulting either in constant confusion of the individual's own values against the demands of family and friends or a harmonious blending of the second and eighth house concerns.

Reacting to the Libran ascendant, these individuals may want to please other people, but find it difficult to accept any ideas at variance with theirs. They need to build up their own image of what they truly accept as important in their lives. Pluto's influence will eventually teach them that free expression of their own individuality is an essential ingredient in any lasting relationship.

Until this happens, these natives may complain

that they have tried unsuccessfully to live up to others' standards. But as they advance steadily toward their goal of mutual sharing with loved ones, they will learn to appreciate not only their own worth but everyone else's as well.

PLUTO IN SCORPIO IN THE THIRD HOUSE

From the third house Scorpio blends the desire to speak profoundly on serious subjects with the Geminian curiosity and need to communicate. Life is an endless quest for knowledge which they want to share with others. In youth, they are naturally reticent, but as they mature, they speak out with self-assurance. They yearn to elicit the thoughts of others, knowing that a thought worth having is a thought worth sharing, and they have the innate ability to understand what others truly mean.

The placement of Mercury must be considered in this situation. Hard aspects may cause tension and blockage resulting in conversational difficulties or speech problems.

These natives have a strong urge to write, to draw out some of the pain and agony of their existence, but exposing innermost thoughts and emotions to the world at large on a printed page infringes upon their sense of privacy. They are unwilling to write down what they feel, turning instead to factual reporting, particularly on topics involving psychology and related fields.

The desire to travel is somewhat diminished here, but when the urge tugs at them occasionally, they may combine business with pleasure on their excursions.

PLUTO IN SCORPIO IN THE FOURTH HOUSE

This configuration endows the native with the solidity of a strong home environment, a respect for family traditions and approval of the parental roles. The father, indicated by the Taurean tenth house, is the disciplinarian in control of the surroundings while the mother, in the fourth, performs effectively her part as homemaker, peacemaker and nurturer. The natives' roots run deep, and as they mature they will seek an alliance with one who can perpetuate the circle of stability.

With Leo on the ascendant, the desire for children will be keen and, with their partner, they will instill in their offspring a sense of discipline, self-reliance, and family loyalty along with a warmth of loving.

They must first establish strong roots within themselves, pruning out those which, becoming gnarled and twisted, may stifle their better qualities with over-possessiveness and a tyrannical approach to discipline. Once rid of these negative influences, they can sustain the family virtues of fidelity, tolerance and love as a bulwark against the cold world.

Through the 1960's and 1970's, much has been written about the disintegration of the modern family. When Pluto is in Scorpio and the fourth house, these people will experience a strong urge to reestablish on a firm foundation the basic tenets of the complete family, with father, mother, children and possibly grandparents, living together in mutual accord and finding their strength as a unit. Such happenings will raise new hopes for the stability of the family and the world.

PLUTO IN SCORPIO IN THE FIFTH HOUSE

Fire and water battle for supremacy here as Scorpio invades Leo's house of romance. Leo delights in speculating, and what is life if not one long and turbulent speculation? None of us is ever certain what lies ahead as we start out on the romantic road, nor are we ever certain how our creations, whether our own children or our artistic endeavors, will ultimately turn out.

This placement enriches these natives with the intense desire to search out every possibility in the compulsion to establish significant relationships. They are inspired by a romantic dream of love and devotion and as they pursue it they may be disappointed on many occasions, but they never relinquish the dream. This combination of the Leo-Scorpio qualities is a hearty endorsement for dreams come true. The romance begun in the fifth house can pave the way in time for establishing seventh house partnerships of a lasting Capricorn nature.

The native's capacity for caring comes from the Cancer ascendant trining the fifth house. This aspect marks them well for the joys and responsibilities of parenthood.

If the fifth house receives favorable aspects from Jupiter, Venus or the Sun, the native might sometime expect a fantastic stroke of luck because of a natural ability to know when to take a chance and when to turn down speculative ventures. But their most rewarding results will come from placing strong values in human companionship as they inspire in others an intense yearning to live life to the fullest. The desire to share their world lights up the fifth house and it glows with the warm embers of true love built upon companionship and understanding.

PLUTO IN SCORPIO IN THE SIXTH HOUSE

In the house of work and service, Pluto natives take their duties seriously, handling jobs in a professional manner and expecting co-workers to do the same. Their friendly, sparkling Geminian ascendant may mislead some fellow employees at first, and relations with them will be valued only if quality and mutual interest in work are shared.

They can make excellent leaders in bringing about safe, fair, productive conditions in the work situation. Having committed themselves to any project, they follow it through to a successful conclusion.

Good health is a primary concern. With no stressful aspects to the sixth house they will have a strong body and will strive to keep in good condition through proper diet and exercise. Hard aspects may bring on problems involving the reproductive organs, or respiratory and nervous disorders. They must learn not to dwell on imaginary illnesses. This aspect also suggests healing abilities which can be used for both physical and psychological improvements.

PLUTO IN SCORPIO IN THE SEVENTH HOUSE

Taurus in the first house and Scorpio in the seventh, two fixed signs, indicate a strong possibility of lasting interpersonal relationships. Scorpio, next door to its own house, blends easily with the Libran concepts, while Gemini in the second and Sagittarius in the eighth suggest a healthy, open-minded value system. Here two individuals can use their intuitive qualities to communicate their sense of self-worth.

The partner may be able to dig out underlying pressures causing uneasiness in the relationship and thus contribute to the growth and renewal of both individuals.

Marriage and other partnerships are highly valued and entered into with the intention of unselfish sharing. Any breach in the contract will probably bring about the death of the relationship.

PLUTO IN SCORPIO IN THE EIGHTH HOUSE

Here is the natural chart with each sign on the cusp of its own house. This factor alone indicates that each house will strongly express its native qualities, unhampered by a mixture of irrelevant characteristics and influenced only by the planet placed therein.

Because of Pluto's great strength here, any stressful aspects to it create serious conflicts for the native. The four cardinal signs falling on the angles bring forth a dynamic individual with a deeply ingrained conception of self-worth who might find it difficult to integrate the values of partnerships. Venus, also at home in the Taurean second house opposing Pluto, creates a see-saw pattern, making compromise necessary for harmony in the native's life. Other planets in square or opposition activate problems over joint resources, legacies and inheritances. It is essential that an open forum of communication and respect for each other's uniqueness is maintained to keep the relationship well-balanced. The Aries-Libra influences can be combined and kept on an equal level. If this does not happen and the native is unable to be tolerant of the partner's point of view, such fixity can cause the end of the association.

Pluto in the eighth also indicates a long healthy life with the vital organs functioning well.

PLUTO IN SCORPIO IN THE NINTH HOUSE

From the ninth house, Pluto in Scorpio tends to increase and intensify the search for knowledge which follows many avenues—religious concepts, metaphysics, psychology, psychiatry, government, the law, the study of foreign lands and cultures. The native becomes a truth-seeker and the truths that are found are shared with humanity on a common, democratic level.

This position gives these natives the ability to be open-minded about all new ideas which come their way. They may be considered radical at times as they explore the mystery of our ingrained social mores which have made us what we are today. The regenerative force of Pluto at work here will inspire them to eradicate antiquated beliefs which have enslaved the human mind for centuries. They realize that the sharing of both abstract philosophies and realistic, concrete plans with other peoples and countries is the most fruitful way of bringing a better life to all humankind.

They particularly enjoy traveling and learning about other cultures first hand. Such understanding of others matures slowly, but with certainty, as they accept the fact that we are not all alike and our basic differences enhance and stimulate our world.

With their sincerity, enthusiasm and integrity they make dedicated teachers in many fields. The Sagittarian talent of talking with others on their level, while at the same time reaching upward to the greater consciousness, will work here to tremendous advantage.

PLUTO IN SCORPIO IN THE TENTH HOUSE

The passion of Scorpio is combined with the ambition of Capricorn as the Saturn-Pluto energies intensify the native's climb to the top. Once they have established in their own minds what their goals are, nothing will daunt them in their drive. In order to achieve prestige and honor which they feel is rightly theirs, they will tear down all obstacles obstructing their path.

In youth the father, austere and forbidding, represented the figure of authority. If this relationship lacked love and understanding, the native may have become compelled on an unconscious level to change into this figure and be recognized in the eyes of the world. This individual must now strive to overcome a basic discomfort in this role so that a manner of ease may be projected.

Their aloofness may sometimes cover up their inherent insecurity, but once they have experienced the vicissitudes of the business world or career fluctuations, they will know intrinsically how they can best use the Scorpio power. Then they will find peace within and success will come their way, but accompanied only with the right set of values.

With fixed signs on the angles they may work

hard to establish a lasting relationship with partners, both business and marital. And because they want these involvements to last forever, they are willing to put all their energies into achieving harmony. In a psychic sense they are building a powerful home in the tenth, for the world is their home.

PLUTO IN SCORPIO IN THE ELEVENTH HOUSE

In Aquarius' house, friendships become vitally important. The cardinal signs, once again, fall on the angles creating a strong individual. Here the native's Scorpio passion involves itself with friendships that are treasured and guarded with zeal.

Their motto is quality, not quantity. Much time and care are expended in choosing those whom they eventually accept into their circle of intimates. Expressing unswerving loyalty, they would willingly die for their friends and in return they expect the same pledge of allegiance from them. In time, the Pluto root-pruning takes the form of discarding from their life those friendships which are no longer valid or of value as they go forward through life.

Because of their popularity and strong personality, these natives are asked to join many organizations. They must decide what is worth-while in these encounters, for the inclination is to assume too many responsibilities and, in spreading themselves too thin, become ineffectual. Their greatest task is to define realistically what they find rewarding in the area of friendships as well as in humanitarian causes.

PLUTO IN SCORPIO IN THE TWELFTH HOUSE

In Neptune's house many conflicting emotions lie under the surface. For peace of mind, the native must first become aware of these conflicts and dredge them up from the darkness of the psyche in order to clear out the negative forces within the soul. If all houses from the seventh on have been met and understood as they should be, the native will find harmony and contentment within the hidden part of self, and their relationships, built up step by step, will be healthy ones. The natural water trine of Pisces, Cancer and Scorpio gives positive expression to the emotions.

In the Virgo-Pisces natural house polarity they will find spiritual peace at last and with the intensity of Scorpio, bring it to fruition in their life. If they have not met responsibilities in contacts with other people through the last seven houses, only unhealthy, frustrating relationships will result. They must intermingle the Virgoan expression of health and service with the Piscean compassion for others. Then, this so-called house of secrets and hidden forces will no longer cause pain.

CHAPTER SIX

NATAL PLUTO IN ASPECT TO NATAL PLANETS

In delineating the effect of Pluto in the natal chart, it is extremely important to consider certain factors:

1. Pluto is most powerful when the natal Sun is in Scorpio.
2. Pluto is powerful when posited in the eighth house.
3. Pluto is powerful when posited on the dynamic angles: first, fourth, seventh and tenth houses. Examples: Pluto in Virgo in the first house; Pluto in Leo in the seventh house. Thus, the sign on any of the four angular houses can be cardinal, fixed or mutable.

Pluto's power is modified somewhat when found in the following situations:

1. Pluto making no strong aspects to other planets.
2. Pluto in strong aspect to another planet which is posited in its own sign. Examples: With Mars in Aries, squaring Pluto in Cancer, Mars would be stronger. With Venus in Taurus,

squaring Pluto in Leo, Venus would be stronger.

With regard to orbs, eight degrees is suggested here.

If Pluto is retrograde, it is on a more subjective level. It will manifest covertly, not overtly. The power to go inside of the self for renewal and regeneration is intensified.

The astrologer should be thoroughly familiar with the meaning of Pluto in each of the five signs discussed herein, thereby eliminating the possibility of confusing the qualities of Pluto in Cancer, for example, with those of Pluto in Leo.

There are times during the life span when Pluto is a mute note in the chart. Its energies are activated with the transits of any of the other nine planets in aspect to its natal degree. The slower-moving planets of Saturn, Uranus and Neptune have a longer-lasting affect upon the native. Also, a generational influence is incorporated to the transits of Uranus and Neptune. The faster-moving planets, i.e. Sun, Moon, Mercury, Venus and Mars, will affect the native's life for a shorter period of time and in a more intimate way.

NATAL PLUTO TO NATAL SUN: Soft Aspects and Positive Potentials

When Pluto's force combines with the Sun's individuality these natives learn easily how to use the power potential. With their dynamic energy, and strength of will, they pattern their life experiences along constructive lines and cope readily with difficulties as they arise. They promptly pull out and discard any weeds which may threaten the health of the seeds they have planted and nurtured, for they understand well when to eliminate the useless and trivial.

They enter into relationships wholeheartedly, knowing what they want and how to get it. Responsibilities in a partnership are met on the basis of equality. But with all, they are concerned that their desires do not infringe upon the rights of others, for they respect their privilege to be themselves. Often they inspire others with their forceful personality, instilling them with the urge to tidy up their own lives and enjoy each day to the fullest. To those they love they are forever loyal, devoted and trustworthy.

At times, when faced with difficult decisions, they may be fearful; yet at the same time they know that they can conquer such fear and handle problems courageously.

The world sees them as creative individuals with a strong sense of integrity and self-respect, needing to be recognized for their talents and sheer abounding strength of positive will.

NATAL PLUTO TO NATAL SUN:
Hard Aspects and Discordant Potentials

In this aspect, the native may perceive one of two extremes: a lack of power or too much power negatively expressed. The placement of the Sun and Pluto in the chart will, of course, indicate in what areas the lack or excess will reveal itself and how it is blocked.

In the first instance, these natives are unaware of the Plutonian power lying dormant within. As they experience life they battle against enormous odds in order to realize their potential. Since Pluto works in subtle ways to get its message across, these individuals may struggle in vain for years. But eventually some event in life will stimulate the hidden resources which heretofore have not been tapped. The lesson in life can be likened to the function of an oil well: a rich supply of the vital fluid lies within, but in order to put it to its proper use, it must be brought to the surface, capped and controlled.

In the other instance, the oil well is gushing full blast at birth. Power is overemphasized and uncontrolled. These individuals grease their path through life, buying their way out of all unpleasantness and refusing to face up to their own personal responsibilities. Or, they may become swaggering bullies, ruthlessly trampling on others' rights and feelings, dominating hordes of people in legitimate business or illegal enterprises. Power possesses them. When the oil well eventually gushes out of control and they are caught in its explosive force, they are compelled to probe into their inner-consciousness for the way to spiritual regeneration.

NATAL PLUTO TO NATAL MOON: Soft Aspects and Positive Potentials

The deep emotions generated here flow smoothly outward in a state of constantly renewed vitality. These natives possess a psychic sensitivity to the powers of regeneration which they use effortlessly to banish destructive habits, improve daily affairs and stimulate growth in their personal relationships. They are fine examples of emotional self-sufficiency based on inner serenity.

The ties to home and family, especially mother, the loyalties to siblings, relatives and friends, freely express their nurturing qualities. Becoming a parent will be a meaningful event in their lives.

The fourth and eighth house influences joining together allow these natives to be unique, while at the same time openly sharing with others in the joy of their individuality. They understand the value of planting firm foundations at home, and recognize the fact that time and care are required to reap the reward of the harvest—a harvest of deep love, affection and family loyalty.

In love affairs, they do not slip easily in and out of involvements but wait patiently for the right person to come along.

They have the ability to help others with emotional problems and situations involving joint finances and resources. Their home is a meeting place for good times with friends, and counseling sessions for those who seek help when in trouble.

NATAL PLUTO TO NATAL MOON:
Hard Aspects and Discordant Potentials

The emotional turmoil aroused by these two planets in a stress aspect can be exceedingly difficult for these natives to understand and control. They are quivering masses of imagined slights, unjustifiable fears, unhealthy dependencies on a parent, and inability to release worn-out relationships. Daily living consists of a series of passionate explosions which generate even more hurt feelings and bruised sensitivities. They must stop forcing their feelings and demands on everyone around them and learn to accept people the way they are, warts and all, or they will be guilty of emotional prostitution at its worst.

Often, to compound the trauma, they may feel alienated from those around them. From childhood they clutch memories and aches which linger on, haunting and wounding their psyche. Why have they allowed these events from the past to torment them, even though the actors in the ancient dramas have long since passed from their sphere? They need a soothing balm to spread on their wounds and the balm can be labeled forgiveness.

These natives need to take a long, hard look at themselves and the emotional shambles in which they live. The Plutonian forces in transit will generate in them the strength and courage to draw out their inner resources for a thorough house cleaning and purging of negative traits. Eventually they can achieve a life of stability and restraint once they find their way and take to heart the old credo, "Let go and let God." For then they will be able to release the past miseries and live completely in the joy of the present.

NATAL PLUTO TO NATAL MERCURY: Soft Aspects and Positive Potentials

Logic and reasoning mark the intellect of these individuals as their penetrating minds delve to the core of the matter and quickly discard irrelevant information. This fortunate combination of energies endows them with the desire to speak with authority on subjects of universal interest. But first they must give it intensive study, probing for the truth, for only when they are thoroughly familiar with a subject will they speak out. If they cannot speak the truth they prefer to remain silent. They gain recognition as ones who know what they are talking about, and their opinions carry substance and weight. When they mount the speaker's platform, their dynamic delivery holds the audience spellbound.

The essence of these two planets, Mercury and Pluto, is shared communication, for knowledge is of no value unless it is shared. With Mercury ruling Gemini and Virgo, these natives are able to use their communicative powers in a practical way, speaking on a level of common interest. Because they are instinctively drawn to their fellow creatures, they are curious to find out all about them—how they live, how they earn a living, what their hobbies and pastimes are. Everything is grist for their computerized mill of knowledge.

NATAL PLUTO TO NATAL MERCURY:
Hard Aspects and Discordant Potentials

The strong desire to communicate may be blocked here and the house positions of Pluto and Mercury will indicate in which area of life this occurs. Dogmatic outbursts from these natives need to be tempered with reason and clear thinking, for they are inclined to trample over other people's ideas and opinions. They can be shrewd, stubborn, harsh and insensitive, speaking mainly from narrow-minded viewpoints. They must learn to consider contrary beliefs carefully instead of carelessly disregarding them, for their way is not the only way.

If their attempts to communicate are constantly frustrated, they may become belligerent and turn to force to make their point. The sign placement of Mercury and Pluto must be carefully analyzed to determine if the aspect will work in an extroverted or introverted way. If, for example, Mercury is in Gemini, and Pluto in Virgo, the Geminian need for versatility and talking with others may be hindered by Virgo's timid approach. If Gemini is the stronger placement the native will have to stop talking long enough to research a project or be considered scatterbrained and superficial. Concentration is often difficult and the mind runs away in many directions.

NATAL PLUTO TO NATAL VENUS: Soft Aspects and Positive Potentials

Venus in the chart determines how one feels about his or her own self-worth, while Pluto determines how one feels about other people's self-worth. The house and sign placement, along with the aspect, will illustrate clearly how the energy can best be channeled. Since Venus is the natural ruler of the second house and Pluto of the eighth house, the give-and-take of the opposition is activated. Consider also that Venus, ruler of the seventh house, is the next-door neighbor of Pluto in the eighth. The planets are ready to exchange their energies in a constructive way.

In their youth, these natives' parents imbued them with confidence, self-respect and a sense of their own value as individuals. As they matured they grew instinctively in awareness and appreciation of others, for they never had to overcome a tangled mess of emotions churning inside.

Their love expression flows freely, ardently, and tenderly. They are truly an inspiration to those whose lives they touch. Their compassion crosses over barriers of class and educational distinctions to be a friend to all.

Close relationships built upon a foundation of equality, trust and acceptance of the values of both people involved will be strong enough to endure throughout a lifetime.

These natives know instinctively how to enjoy all the good things. They surround themselves with beautiful objects, creating a tranquil environment and adorning themselves with gorgeous clothing and jewelry. The Taurean qualities enable them to delight in color, texture, shape, balance and line, which they enthusiastically embrace and incorporate into their life-style.

NATAL PLUTO TO NATAL VENUS: Hard Aspects and Discordant Potentials

The native's sense of self-worth lies buried in confusion.

Obstacles beyond these natives' control, such as deprivation in childhood, constant parental criticism, and a lack of love, may have undermined their confidence and self-esteem. Unfortunate long-range effects of fault-finding and discontent emerge later on in their adult relationships. Since the parents did not find them to be worthy, they automatically feel that they are not and, therefore, no one else will find them worthy, either. They try hard to be what everyone else expects them to be and often end up frustrated and insecure, hiding behind an emotional roadblock, unable to let their own personality shine through, unable to express love.

Although their behavioral patterns may be distorted, much can be changed in their lives through the force of Pluto transits. Pluto, taking away that part which is no longer needed, forces these individuals to take stock of themselves. They may be plunged into emotional catastrophes which compel them to review their value system. In breaking away from the chains that bind them in their narrow world, they may ultimately reach upward for the greatest goal of all: realization of their own individuality. As they regenerate themselves, they will then attract those who will demand neither too much nor too little, but who allow them the chance to function as a whole person in charge of their own destiny. Many delights will come their way; not only the capacity to share a love unfettered by fear, but also the opportunity to discover the joy of the Taurean appreciation of fine arts in their daily lives.

NATAL PLUTO TO NATAL MARS: Soft Aspects and Positive Potentials

The energy of Mars combined with Pluto is generally considered to be the most dynamic aspect in planetary interplay. The powerful inward thrust of the native is funneled into perpetual renewal and constructive use.

Mars is energy, action, force, and power—a different kind of power than Pluto's, which is hidden, inner, subtle. The combination of Mars' fire and Pluto's water can be compared to the dynamos in a huge dam. The rush of the water flowing in through controlled channels generates the creation of electricity and is released for the world to consume. Another analogy comes to mind in the fire box originally used in locomotives. Burning wood or coal heated the water which turned into steam to run the massive engines. Or consider an ordinary battery which will run down unless it is constantly recharged. Here individuals are their own rechargers, extracting energy from a limitless supply deep within.

All this boundless vitality at their command is expended with confidence. By putting one foot in front of the other, always moving forward, they know exactly where they are going. They brim over with enthusiasm and work tirelessly toward their goals. Their relations with others run smoothly, for they are ever willing to help, not only with their strong physicial body (on moving day), but with fearlessness in the face of obstacles. They are true friends, offering help when needed, but seldom meddling in others' affairs.

NATAL PLUTO TO NATAL MARS: Hard Aspects and Discordant Potentials

Natives with this aspect may experience two reactions; either they feel tired and have a low energy level, or they have a high energy level that is wasted in a scattering of forces. This fire-water combination with its potential for destruction must be handled carefully. Its expression will depend on which planet has the upper hand. Mars in Aries, stronger in its own sign, squaring Pluto in Cancer, may win out because of one's urgency to act. But, on the other hand, the Cancer security-drives, and feelings of sensitivity may deny the urge to action for fear of losing something of value.

So these natives withdraw into a shell, vacillating between these extremes—the need to act and the fear of action, thus locking themselves in a corner.

Mars in Scorpio and Pluto in Leo activate another fire-water cross play. These individuals often create their own frustrations. Wrapped up in their emotions, they worry about what others think of them. Nothing gets solved. The fire and water generate steam, which dissipates, and the natives find themselves contemplating their conflicts while sitting in a steam bath of their own making.

With Mars in Taurus and Pluto in Leo, two fixed signs, the ego is affected. Taurus is concerned with self-worth and Leo with self-image. Neither one is giving in. Taureans want to attain what others have in a material sense so the world will think well of them. Their ambition could run rampant, turning them into bullies who make impulsive decisions with no consideration for the rights of others. Such activity shows misuse of energy either in overworking or in counter-productive action.

In another sense, Pluto-in-Libra square Mars-in-Cancer produces blockage. Strong partners would dominate in relationships and the native, resenting the domination, would nevertheless allow it to happen.

NATAL PLUTO TO NATAL JUPITER: Soft Aspects and Positive Potentials

A combination of eighth and ninth house qualities arouses a high degree of spiritual evolvement.

Some may consider these individuals unorthodox in their precepts as they reach for a higher attunement than the commonly accepted beliefs of organized religion. They penetrate through its vagueness and inconsistencies, unaffected by its hellfire-and-brimstone concepts and its stress on original sin and eternal damnation. They simply are not buying this in the stark realism of today's world. With their strong faith, they tap into a greater source of inspiration and spirituality which gradually leads to an unshakable understanding of what religion is truly meant to be.

Every individual is unique in their estimation, and they communicate easily with all in a discussion of moral beliefs. They stick to their code of ethics in respecting and evaluating the rights of others to believe as they wish.

Highly educated, first through books and later through world travel, they constantly seek truth in all matters that come their way. Their philosophical teachings cover a broad concept of social responsibility for all fellow beings.

With the ninth house need to communicate, they speak out to everyone within their sphere. They feel strongly that most of the world's problems could be solved if people, as well as their leaders, talked together openly, frankly, without hypocrisy and guile.

Always boundlessly optimistic and generous, they have the capabilities needed for fine spiritual leaders. They look forward to the highest possibilities that humankind can reach as they make ready to accept the transformation which will be experienced when Pluto regenerates from the deepest level of all.

NATAL PLUTO TO NATAL JUPITER: Hard Aspects and Discordant Potentials

These natives may suffer from inner turmoil, for they may not have established a workable code of conduct to follow in life. Bombarded on all sides by rapidly shifting standards and blatant permissiveness in sexual freedom, crime at all levels, bribery, corruption and questionable ethics in business and government, they know not where to turn. To cover their confusion they try to impress upon others their importance and expound uncertain philosophical ideas and religious concepts. Usually they have not studied these subjects in depth and slide along on surface knowledge, forcing viewpoints on unwilling listeners. They may become a nuisance with their bombastic opinions and invasions of privacy on such intimate subjects as religion, politics and personal morals. They fancy themselves as leaders, teachers, gurus, spreading the word to humankind; however, in reality, they may be pompous bores.

When events turn out disastrously, they find it difficult to accept their responsibility, trying instead to put the blame on others. In the negative Jupiterian sense they do it all too much, too often, too loudly. They suffer from tunnel vision: their view is the only view; their way is the only way. Some crashing catastrophe in their lives will sooner or later force them to look to their inner, hidden resources. The path to their potential spirituality will then open up.

With Pluto in Cancer and Jupiter in Capricorn, a conflict is created over the strength of the traditional mother-father role. Which one is in charge here? The native may be confused since childhood over the seesaw pattern of the Plutonian renewal forces fighting it out with the traditional Capricorn qualities. Consider also the Cancerian emotion, always easily aroused, battling it out with the Saturnian discipline which wants only to marshall energies into a neat and tidy line.

In another example consider Pluto-in-Leo, identified with love and romance, opposite Jupiter in Aquarius which expresses love in a detached, Platonic style. They are looking in different directions with divergent viewpoints. Leo says, "How much is in it for me?" and Aquarius wonders, "How much can I give the world?" In order to live in harmony, the native must somehow learn to balance this seesaw.

NATAL PLUTO TO NATAL SATURN: Soft Aspects and Positive Potentials

The time cycle of Saturn and the renewal forces of Pluto endow these natives with a well-developed sense of responsibility in the practical affairs of life. They take their duties seriously and build constructively for present and future needs.

The eighth and tenth house coupling instills leadership qualities based upon careful consideration of others' resources and values. They know that mutual respect and cooperation are necessary for any effective organizational effort to occur. When the time is ripe, they can release outmoded institutional programs and work toward something newer and better. They are fine leaders because they consider the character and personality of each person and intuitively understand how to encourage their capabilities.

Their profound patience in all endeavors stands them in good stead throughout their life. Instinctively, they know that anything of lasting worth is built slowly and carefully. Shoddy workmanship has no place in their plans, and they take steps immediately to eliminate it. The Saturn influence erects its foundations on solid ground and planned obsolescence has no part in it.

With the water-earth combination complementing each other, their interest in ecology surges to the front, for they abhor waste and the wanton destruction of our natural resources. Water feeding earth brings forth carefully controlled abundance which they can channel toward humankind's advantage.

NATAL PLUTO TO NATAL SATURN: Hard Aspects and Discordant Potentials

The combination of Saturn's pressure with Pluto's intensity compels those individuals to work out problems in their life. The sense of timing is thrown out of balance and extra caution is required in order to avoid the danger of action at an inappropriate time. Thus, this aspect could cause fear of taking any action at any time.

Leadership abilities can be thwarted by obstacles beyond these natives' control. Sooner or later, when frustration wears down their vitality, depression and apathy move in. In the early part of life, negative conditioning from the father or an authority figure may set the stage later on for outbursts of rebellion and expressions of deep-seated fears. It is their task to learn to release the pent-up energy created by stress and channel it into a reservoir of self-respect. They should look for better and better role models in which to pattern their ideal of authority.

Their survival depends on overcoming obstacles thrown in their path. Ultimately, under the impact of the Plutonian renewal, they will learn that the desirable qualities will surface from the depths. Then, through disciplined endeavor and hard-won experience they will move forward to enjoy their tangible results.

The aspect of Pluto-in-Cancer squre Saturn-in-Libra, may have one of two effects. In childhood, the father's heavy-handed discipline over the family may have created turmoil and resentment in the home; or, the mother may have held sway, laying down rigid rules of behavior. When children grow up under these unfortunate conditions, later in their lives as they reach out to the seventh house, they will oftentimes attract someone who will fit into and fulfill this pattern of dependency already established.

Another example might involve Pluto-in-Virgo square Saturn-in-Gemini. Here the serious-minded Virgos cannot enjoy life because they concentrate on practical details too much. They may have brilliant minds with a need to share ideas, but they become so completely immersed in daily work that their conversation revolves around details of office routine. To break out of this rut they must learn to communicate freely with others, listening to what they have to say and taking a sincere interest in their problems. On the other hand, if Gemini dominates the square, they would be excessively talkative and, consequently, bores.

NATAL PLUTO TO NATAL URANUS: Soft Aspects and Positive Potentials

The Uranian urge for freedom and the Plutonian regenerational force, eighth and eleventh house affairs, merge together in a positive union, each bringing out the best of the other. Sudden, disruptive changes can be taken in stride and absorbed into daily life with a minimum of stressful reaction. These natives thrive on a program of variety and excitement.

This combination allows for a unique blending of genius and emotional consciousness which can tune into higher planes of social concepts that endorse humanitarianism in its most exalted form. It dares to search for newer ways to extend the ladder of evolvement, from the mundane to the ultimate, in human potential.

The eleventh house represents love received, while the eighth house signifies the way other people in one's life feel about themselves. The positive aspects indicate that these individuals value themselves highly and are able to exhibit their sense of worthiness by freely giving love and friendship. In its highest sense of sharing, it represents a give-and-take quality that encourages individual growth and freedom. True love and true friendship also are manifested in their ability to let go, when the time comes, of another, so that that person may pursue their growth potential and happiness in a new direction.

NATAL PLUTO TO NATAL URANUS: Hard Aspects and Discordant Potentials

Because they lack a strong sense of identity, these natives create problems in their relationships. They lean heavily upon others to fill voids within themselves. In time, such relationships wear thin, putting the emotional stability of both parties under strain. If either planet aspects a personal planet in the chart, the stress will be intensified. Such a situation may bring on sudden Uranian partings and Plutonian upheavals. Unless other areas of the chart offer help, such events can leave lifelong scars upon these natives.

It is essential for growth that they realize the differences in what friendships offer. One can be, in effect, a cup of poison while another is a cup of soothing, bracing tea. One can offer growth, while another can tear away at their shreds of self-respect. These individuals need to find friends who can bolster their frail and battered egos by instilling self-confidence and a firm belief in their own talents and abilities. They need to purge from their lives those who find unhealthy satisfaction in their constant dependency and servitude.

With Uranus-in-Aries and Pluto-in-Cancer, a conflict arises over the need for freedom and the need for closeness. The explosive Aries tramples over the Cancer vulnerability and constant friction in life is fomented. Only when these natives work at appreciating their own value as individuals and no longer allow others to intimidate and control them, will this paradox be solved.

The Pluto-in-Leo square Uranus-in-Taurus accents the fixity of both signs. Leo demands identity but Taurus prefers to lie back and take life easy in the porch swing. Both Pluto and Uranus are out of their natural elements here and working at cross-purposes. The house placements in the chart will indicate how the tension can best be resolved.

NATAL PLUTO TO NATAL NEPTUNE: SEXTILE ASPECT ONLY

Most astrologers agree that the sextile aspect represents opportunity. Here is opportunity unparalled in the history of the world as the two most distant planets, Neptune, presently in Sagittarius, and Pluto, presently in Libra, first settled into this position in 1940, and will remain so until the end of the century and beyond. Never before has humanity, with its powerful telescopes, had the chance to observe such a phenomenon in the heavens, while at the same time feeling its effects upon the earth plane.

Consider the interweaving of the energies involved: Plutonian renewal, Neptunian inspiration, Scorpio intensity, Piscean compassion, Libran equality and justice and the Sagittarian search for wisdom. It would seem that the clouds that have blanketed the skies and humankind's progress for centuries are now lifting and the light of illumination is shining through. Humankind is at last confronted with the chance to open up its heart and mind with concern for its fellow creatures; to recognize and accept all diverse forms of religion and government; to foster equality among all, regardless of race or sex; and to seek to educate each person for an awareness of greater accomplishment and spiritual awakening in the wonder and potential goodness of the human race.

A well-known quotation of uncertain origin expresses this well and brings it down to a personal level: "A friend is one who knows you as you are, understands where you have been, accepts what you have become and still, gently, invites you to grow." Under these powerful planetary influences, the world can not only grow, but can leap forward as Pluto and Neptune, harnessed together and entwined in harmony, valiantly pull us all from our battered earth toward the ultimate splendor waiting beyond the horizon.

BOOK TWO
PLUTO IN TRANSIT

CHAPTER SEVEN

TRANSITING PLANETS TO NATAL PLUTO

In considering the action of transiting planets to natal Pluto, the following points should be considered.

When the fast-moving planets (i.e. Sun, Moon, Mercury, Venus and Mars) transit natal Pluto, the effect is acute, but temporal. The Sun, which never retrogrades, passes over natal Pluto once a year and projects its influence for approximately three days approaching and three days leaving. The rapidly moving Moon, which also never retrogrades, travels over Pluto once a month in a matter of hours, causing at most, a minor emotional experience. Mercury and Venus, if not in retrograde motion, also pass over Pluto yearly, activating a short-lived response. Mars' stay is somewhat longer, and when in retrograde motion over Pluto's natal degree, will be felt more sharply.

The slower moving planets concentrate their influences more intensely. Jupiter, in one sign for a year, can be in exact aspect to Pluto for two months or more if it is retrograding over the degree involved. Otherwise, if direct, its passage takes about one month. Saturn's visits last for two or three months if going direct, but in retrograde motion can hit Pluto three times in one year, making its effect emphatic. Uranus, because of long periods of retrogradation in its seven year cycle, can hover over a natal degree for about four years. The combination of Uranus and Pluto can be the most dramatic and startling of all. Neptune, in its fifteen year transit with long retrograde periods, throws its subtle influence over only two or three degrees a year. Thus, its effect can be activated for as long as five years.

Therefore, in order to delineate the effect of these aspects as wisely as possible, the student should bear in mind that the influence of a transiting planet to the natal Pluto placement is always tempered by the speed of its motion and whether it is retrograde or direct.

TRANSITING SUN TO NATAL PLUTO

Soft Aspects and Positive Potentials

This three to four day period can be used beneficially by encouraging possibilities previously overlooked. The Sun beams positive rays and, aligning itself with the depth of Pluto to penetrate and strengthen will-power, purges the self of accumulated and unneccessary residue. The time is ripe for renewing old relationships that can warm the heart, for making good impressions on new acquaintances and for taking any affirmative action called for in the daily routine.

Hard Aspects and Discordant Potentials

If these natives have neglected essential details and are walking around with their heads wrapped up in egotism, they will find that their feet stumble over tricky obstacles along the road. If they insist on their own way, they will run headlong into disappointments. It would benefit them to seek knowledge of their own inner motives, rather than trying to coerce others into following their commands.

TRANSITING MOON TO NATAL PLUTO

Soft Aspects and Positive Potentials

This brief period should be used as a time to rest, relax emotionally, and tune in to the body. If these natives work fast enough they can settle old disputes, make amends for misunderstandings and start happy new relationships. It is an opportune time to seek assistance from some woman important in the life, for she should respond generously.

Another suggestion for using this short period productively is in cleaning house in a practical, soap-and-water way. The results of using this increased emotional energy in such a manner will be rewarding.

Hard Aspects and Discordant Potentials

If one feels depressed and drained, he or she can be assured that the influence will be short lived. Taking a few hours off for a nap which will banish the Excedrin headache and renew vitality is the most sensible action to take.

TRANSITING MERCURY TO NATAL PLUTO

Soft Aspects and Positive Potentials

Answers can comc to problems not solvable before as the mind perks along with deep, well-ordered thoughts. All forms of communication are expressed clearly and to the native's advantage. One is able to talk over problems with others, speak in a crisp, clear manner in public, and write smoothly as well.

It is an excellent time to plan trips, research projects, and to be in contact with people whose companionship is enjoyable.

Hard Aspects and Discordant Potentials

If the natives' thoughts are confused and over-stimulated, then they should avoid verbal fights, erratic speech, or blurting out harsh and vindictive statements. Conversely, they can become moody, sensitive, sulky and uncommunicative, retreating into silence. Neither course of action is desirable. If aware of this transit, individuals should hold off until it passes before starting any new projects or committing themselves verbally to any personal or business undertakings.

TRANSITING VENUS TO NATAL PLUTO

Soft Aspects and Positive Potentials

The natives should take advantage of this transit, when their charisma is blooming, to plan a big party or accept social invitations from friends. They will appear at their best in new attractive clothing, sexual magnetism oozing from every pore. Members of the opposite sex will flock around to bask in their allure and happy times will reign.

In this situation watch for the conjunction, two sextiles and two trines during the year. It is an excellent time to plan for parties.

Hard Aspects and Discordant Potentials

Here we have the opposite as above. The native may choose to curl up in a blue funk, slop around in old clothes, and refuse to socialize with anyone. They feel that they would be lucky to be invited anyway, for no doubt they would spill their drink on the rug and burn a cigarette hole in the hostess' new draperies. They feel at odds with the whole world and just want to be left alone to brood and contemplate their miseries.

TRANSITING MARS TO NATAL PLUTO

Soft Aspects and Positive Potentials

With this interplay, physical energy surges through the individual, activating him or her to tackle projects involving stamina and strength. Now is the time for house painting, gardening, unpacking cartons, cleaning out the garage or organizing amateur ball games. Any restlessness should be poured into constructive group endeavors.

One may also, at this time, give vent to enthusiasms which are usually carefully controlled. Their candor and straightforwardness openly expressed are a refreshing delight to everyone around them.

Hard Aspects and Discordant Potentials

On the other hand, energy may go on a rampage here. Individuals may wear themselves out by overdoing physically, not knowing when to stop and rest. Or they may become obnoxious and aggressive to close friends, demanding that everything be done their way, as they trample roughly on the sensitivities of others. They may pick fights over the slightest misunderstanding, even to the point of dragging up some long-forgotten incident to battle over. They can be obsessed with speed and violent action. It is imperative that they curb these dangerous self-defeating forces at this time.

TRANSITING JUPITER TO NATAL PLUTO

Soft Aspects and Positive Potentials

Since this aspect lasts approximately one month, the individual has ample opportunity to use the Jupiterian energy advantageously. Previously made plans, from which one can benefit greatly, can now come to fruition. Long overdue financial debts can be paid off and, likewise, other monies will come in, enabling the individual to take care of obligations.

In their personal life, happiness and optimism abound as loved ones gather round to enjoy the good things of life.

Hard Aspects and Discordant Potentials

Under these aspects, individuals may be inclined to overdo everything as optimism runs wild. They turn into spendthrifts and gamblers, laying out expansive plans which have little possibility of attaining reality. They go to extremes trying to impress everyone with their own importance, talking big and puffing on pipe dreams. Here is the famous example of the person with the champagne taste and the beer pocketbook.

TRANSITING SATURN TO NATAL PLUTO

Soft Aspects and Positive Potentials

With this transit, individuals earn the results of the patience and hard work they have poured into long-range plans and committments. It is a time of accomplishment and also an excellent time to begin new projects. They may obtain valuable advice and financial aid from an older person now, one who can advise on tax matters, insurance, blue chip investments and real estate transactions. Under Saturn's tutelage they will be able to structure their careers wisely, marshall ambitions in the right direction, and adhere closely to the finest ethical standards.

Hard Aspects and Discordant Potentials

When the onset of this transit hits, individuals should try their best to understand what is happening. They may encounter frustrations on every corner, heavy responsibilities, delays in career matters, a drop in income, or insufficient funds to inaugurate new plans. When these pressures sink in they will probably feel worried, depressed and unable to cope. In severe cases they may become neurotic. If they understand that this, too, shall pass away in time, it will give them renewed energy and hope to ride out the tide.

It is most important that they brace themselves to meet their responsibilities and obligations, no matter what the cost. They may feel that their back is to the wall and there is no way to turn, but if they use the finest forces of Saturn and Pluto, they can stick it out and be much finer individuals when the transit is over.

TRANSITING URANUS TO NATAL PLUTO

Soft Aspects and Positive Potentials

The planet of the unexpected comes here to visit the planet of that which is established. Inevitably there is disruption and change for these natives, but, it can be a welcome disruption, trading the old for the new, making necessary alterations in the fabric of their lives. They may usher in these changes with delighted surprise, accepting them eagerly with an open mind.

Their intuitive knowledge of others can interact in a positive way. They feel that many possibilities formerly overlooked are now available to them if they take assertive action. This is particularly true in career matters for it spurs them to leave jobs they may dislike, and to find something more suited to their abilities.

The only conjunction to be considered here occurred in Virgo from 1961 to 1969. These children therefore experienced the conjunction when still quite young.

Uranus in Pisces from 1919 to 1928 trined natal Pluto in Cancer. These natives were also young at the time, some of them in their teens. Uranus in Scorpio from 1974 to 1981 trines natal Pluto in Cancer during the native's adult years.

Hard Aspects and Discordant Potentials

In its long holding pattern in square aspect, transiting Uranus touches off the dynamite which shakes the Plutonian slowness into open action. Whatever Pluto has been subtly working on, now erupts to the surface of the natives' life and, faced with a devastating blow they must struggle to adjust to its sweeping dramatic changes. They find themselves on an untrodden pathway under conditions that are disruptive, but at the same time bringing them a kind of freedom never experienced before. Can they handle it wisely? Can they work with these forces in a positive way so that the turbulent emotions aroused will not explode? They must prime themselves to start again on their interrupted journey with a different, fresh outlook for they will realize in time that what Pluto destroyed in the life resulted in a necessary and perhaps violent deliverance.

Only three squares are formed during this period: Transiting Uranus in Aries from 1927 to 1935 squares natal Pluto in Cancer; transiting Uranus in Libra from 1968 to 1974 squares natal Pluto in Cancer; transiting Uranus in Scorpio from 1974 to 1981 squares natal Pluto in Leo.

TRANSITING NEPTUNE TO NATAL PLUTO

Soft Aspects and Positive Potentials

During this transit, natives will expand their awareness to a greater understanding of the mysteries of the universe. It is an excellent time to study subjects dealing with mind expansion, the occult, astrology, metaphysics or any related topics. They will also be inspired in the realm of music and the visual arts.

Since this is a long-lasting transit, individuals under its effect will be awakened to the deep compulsions within the secret self. Some of these may be harmful and they struggle to identify and cleanse them from their psyche. Other yearnings which may lead them to fulfill their potential can now be encouraged and expanded for their greater good.

Any deceptions which may have been shadow-boxing in the back of their heads are now brought out in the open and dealt with. If they have felt themselves to be victims in the past or been exploited by others, they can now purge these negative influences from their lives.

At the end of this transit these natives will have undergone a spiritual renewal and greater understanding of themselves. All of these energies will merge into a feeling of control over their ultimate destiny.

Hard Aspects and Discordant Potentials

Individuals may now suffer from strange, deeply imbedded tensions haunting them from the past. These tensions may be difficult to identify, for they keep slipping away into the Neptunian mists. The individuals feel blocked and frustrated by these nameless emotions and, as a result, may lapse into lethargy and depression, retreating from reality and seeking solace in alcohol or drugs.

They may also seek compensation for this situation in attempting to exercise power, either consciously or unconsciously, over those close to them. It is as if they are grasping at something, they know not what, trying to get some control into their existence.

At this time it is important for them to handle their financial affairs in an orderly, disciplined fashion, or they may find this part of the life is also fraught with deception. They can easily become the victim of a fast-talking con-artist who spirits money away from them before they realize what happened.

If these natives can weather the mists and storm clouds of this transit, hanging on and using the strong Plutonian influences to overcome the illusions and delusions of Neptune, they will inevitably learn what to avoid in the future and what qualities to encourage in their daily lives.

CHAPTER EIGHT
TRANSITING PLUTO TO THE NATAL PLACEMENTS

In an average lifetime, transiting Pluto in its slow motion will conjunct only those planets which are in the next four or five signs ahead of its natal place. As it travels through these houses it throws sextiles, squares, trines and oppositions to the other natal planets.

Pluto making a conjunction to another natal planet can be compared to the impact of a gentleman who arrives for a lengthy stay, leaves his signature in the guest book, rearranges the furniture, cleans out the attic and the basement and, when he finally departs, has altered forever the values, life style and commitments of the hosts.

To Pluto, a sextile is similar to a next-door neighbor who is unobtrusive, friendly and cooperative. The trine represents the neighbor who actively participates in our life, and when she borrows a cup of sugar, brings in return the whole cake. A square describes a neighbor whose property abuts ours and who causes tension in ceaseless complaints about Pluto's rubbish blowing over in their yard or our weeds straggling under the fence. The opposition is the fellow across the street who keeps us awake with loud parties and barking dogs, but who cheerfully lends the lawn mower or gives us a lift to work when it rains.

Bearing in mind that each sign has thirty degrees and that Pluto transited Cancer in twenty-six years, Leo in nineteen, Virgo in fourteen and Libra in thirteen, it is obvious that the power planet lingers a long time over each degree and, in retrograde motion, can cross a particular degree three times. It is generally conceded in such cases that events and changes are activated on the first impact, brought to a time of decision on the second and to a final conclusion on the third. Such motion may take as long as four years back and forth over a degree.

Pluto, in its inevitable journey and its once-in-a-lifetime visit, leaves its mark on the native. Its importance can never be overlooked or underestimated. Due to its subtle, intense nature, the native will become aware of its effects gradually. But once Pluto has made its station, the affairs of that house and sign will never be the same. A positive aspect clears the way for a happier, more fulfilling life. Any challenging aspect from Pluto can inflict one with pain and agony during the transit, but once it is over and the pathway is clear, the individual will have met the challenge in a stirring rebirth and as a result, becomes a finer human being.

Transiting Pluto in Libra Conjunct Natal Sun in Libra

The inborn Libran qualities of justice, fair play and equality are activated during this transit. In their daily lives these natives are confronted with situations in which these conditions are brought forcefully to their attention, either in employment, business dealings or relationships at home. The transit dramatizes the necessity for solving some of the age-old problems confronting us all: equal opportunity in careers, equal pay for women, blacks and minority groups, and a cleaning out of unfair practices in the tax system, the courts and government. These individuals can be greatly aroused by the multitudinous difficulties waiting to be resolved, and with the Plutonian power pushing them along they are inspired to do something about these problems.

Transiting Pluto in Libra Trine Natal Sun in Gemini

This transit, activating a new cycle in the native's life, opens doors to the use of creative abilities and latent potentials which may have been stifled or stunted before. Geminian qualities of curiosity and communication are energized toward working in harmony with others—a harmony based upon mutual esteem for their uniqueness as individuals. New projects started at this time can be expected to attain long-range goals.

Transiting Pluto in Libra Trine Natal Sun in Aquarius

This is an excellent time for individuals to welcome into their life the subtle changes which Pluto can bring about. They will be motivated to eliminate the outworn, the shoddy and the useless from their daily existence and move forward to the acceptance of a finer set of values and a healthy growth in transition.

The combined intellect of two air signs works harmoniously here toward a brighter future. These natives have the chance to put any Aquarian ideas, however startling they may seem, to productive use. They have the potential to diagnose the ills of humankind, and by using democratic processes, arrive at intelligent, workable solutions.

Transiting Pluto in Libra Square Natal Sun in Cancer

Individuals going through this transit must struggle to overcome a loss of confidence in themselves. Feelings of depression and lack of ambition may haunt them as they try to understand the identity crisis which now confronts them. Primarily, it is a tug of war between their Cancerian need for dependency and the closeness of the family, and their desire for total commitment to one other person. Are they involved with many or are they involved with just one? The situation may appear hopeless or deadlocked but they must steel themselves to hang on, build up their ego feelings and ride out the challenges. Some event will point out the need to eliminate over-dependency and manipulation with those close to them, thus allowing them a measure of freedom to be their own person. Then, this phase of life will bring a substantial growth in their character.

Transiting Pluto in Libra Square Natal Sun in Capricorn

Here individuals undergo strong urges to move along in career, balanced by equally felt needs for close relationships in their lives. Which will become more important? They know they cannot accomplish it all on their own, yet they are fearful of too much dependency on others. During this transit, they will experience the pain and frustration of the problem, but once it has passed, they will have learned how to best manage these two energies for their own peace of mind.

Transiting Pluto in Libra Opposing Natal Sun in Aries

While this transit is occurring, subtle changes take place in the natives' value system. They ponder the importance of loved ones in their lives, as opposed to the price of selfhood. They know they must seek human companionship, yet they want to hold on to their own individuality. Pluto puts the personal brake on their energies, making them realize that they cannot always go it alone, that others can help and that they can, on occasion, ask others to do so. Until they learn this particular Plutonian lesson, they will not be in harmony within themselves and their environment.

Transiting Pluto in Libra Conjunct Natal Moon in Libra

This transit has a powerful and purging effect upon the native's emotions as it brings up for review personal relationships, particularly those with women. It sets in motion the desire to cut loose from unions which have become stifling or binding and to prepare for deep changes in close attachments. It often signals the end of marriage or love affairs which are no longer meaningful and satisfying, while at the same time it brings about solutions to other difficult emotional problems.

These individuals are now physically tuned in to others. In career matters, they can benefit in all relations with the public, since this aspect encourages them to sense as well as solve troublesome situations.

Since Moon-in-Libra individuals have been conditioned in childhood to be concerned about the needs of others along with their own needs, they now have the opportunity to integrate the two demands. Essentially, they do not want to be alone; they must have significant others around to fulfill their life. They now put much emphasis upon relating by reflecting out to others as others reflect back to them in a healthy emotional exchange.

Transiting Pluto in Libra Trine Natal Moon in Gemini

Here Pluto adds stability to the fluctuating Geminian Moon. The natives' usual impulse to expend nervous energy by darting off in all directions is now steadied and subdued. Interest in others now is genuine, not superficial, as their conversation takes on more weight. Their considerable talents in communicating can be utilized in writing, teaching, and speaking on serious subjects which may have previously been overlooked or scorned.

In personal relationships they learn to refrain from too much talking and constant verbal analysis of their every move. They are able to respond with more understanding and to share feelings on a deeper level with loved ones. At the same time, following the Plutonian urges, they spend many hours in quiet introspection in a desire to know themselves better.

Transiting Pluto in Libra Trine Natal Moon in Aquarius

The combination of these two signs in fortunate interplay is an excellent example of emotional democracy. The Aquarian person has a commitment to non-possessive love, the kind which understands that it is possible to love more than one person at a time in different ways. The Libran influence shows the joys of being intimately involved with only one. Here the Plutonian qualities intensify the emotions of the two air signs and lead the way to an appreciation of close bonds without the possessiveness and manipulation of which Libra has sometimes been guilty.

Transiting Pluto in Libra Square Natal Moon in Cancer

At this time, the natives may feel their emotions are stagnating like dirty water as they wallow in self-pity and feelings of frustration. Moods shift quickly and they shut themselves off from friends and family. They may feel emotionally heavy, depressed and sluggish, unable to respond positively to those around them. They may be guilty of whining and nagging. Financial difficulties and unexpected expenses rise up to plague them. All in all, it is not a happy time.

Basically, the emotions are dammed up. This condition may be caused by traumatic events in childhood from which they have never found release. With Pluto stirring up inner turmoil it is imperative that they seek a healthy adjustment to all the negative forces bombarding them. Only through careful analysis of their deep emotional blocks and the understanding and acceptance of the Plutonian catalyst, will they find the answer to a more rewarding life.

Transiting Pluto in Libra Square Natal Moon in Capricorn

Under this transit the natives' business orientation will be brought into stress by the influx of feeling and the intellectual approach generated by Pluto in Libra. They are forced to decide which of these two crucial factors—career or loved ones—is more important to their well-being. Capricorn derives much pleasure and satisfaction from business success, while Libra needs an emotional alliance with another to feel fulfilled. Which one will be the stronger? They may undergo some kind of upheaval at this time which will allow them to learn to live with both of these qualities well-balanced in their lives.

Transiting Pluto in Libra Opposing Natal Moon in Aries

The Moon-in-Aries natives have thus far been going through life expressing their emotions independently from the reaction of others. They feel what they want to feel, openly and above-board, with concern only for themselves. Now Libra, the sign of partnerships, demands that they consider the emotional sensibilities of those close to them and come to a compromise. They cannot be well-adjusted persons being wholly wrapped up in self, nor wholly dependent on another for emotional feedback. Now is the time in their life when they must learn to balance the two factors.

Transiting Pluto in Libra Conjunct Natal Mercury in Libra

The insights stimulated by this transit can be utilized most effectively by exercising the mind in healthy competition with others of equal or greater intellect. Now these individuals pursue many forms of knowledge and in so doing realize that life is an ongoing process combining past, present and future.

All manner of resources which may have been unavailable in the past, are now theirs for the asking. Partnership agreements can be formed under fortunate conditions. In career, they can move steadily ahead if they have done their work well.

The natives' concern for others is intensified. They care deeply about the responses and thoughts of important persons in their life and seek to relate harmoniously on all levels. It is an excellent aspect for counseling or other psychologically helpful services. Their keen ability to get quickly to the root of their anxieties is sharpened now for they know instinctively not only how others feel, but also how they think.

Transiting Pluto in Libra Trine Mercury in Gemini

Mercury in its own sign, Gemini, is powerful and the natives' need to communicate can be used productively in whatever career they choose. If they lean towards writing, this is the time for them to settle down seriously at the typewriter, for their thoughts will flow freely and much will be accomplished. They make excellent arbitrators now for they understand both sides of the question and know how to resolve it with fairness and understanding.

In approaching strangers, they sense how to put them at ease and establish an immediate rapport, a valuable attribute in both social and business life.

Transiting Pluto in Libra Trine Mercury in Aquarius

This fortunate combination of energies sharpens and focuses the native's mind to a degree of brilliance from which they can surely benefit. Old concepts and new ideas can be blended together to reinforce the best parts of each. They are now spurred on to use the democratic process in any problems connected with racism or sexism which may enter daily life. With Aquarian detachment they can come up with practical solutions in order to work out these situations, helping each individual to attain what is rightfully his or hers.

Transiting Pluto in Libra Square Natal Mercury in Cancer

Mental stagnation can possibly occur now, causing these individuals to sit idly by, unable to perform their duties. They may become fuss-budgets preoccupied with minute details while important information slides by. They can turn into incessant whiners, irritating their family and nagging their friends with a list of complaints on their shortcomings. Nothing seems to go right and their popularity sinks to an all-time low.

In this case, individuals must examine thoroughly their responses to those who are close to them and take steps to improve relationships. If they have been expecting too much, now is the time to discuss the difficulties in plain words and clear-cut communication.

Transiting Pluto in Libra Square Natal Mercury in Capricorn

Mental depression brought on by discontent at work may require a change in life-style or the services of a counselor to help these natives understand and overcome the obstacles which are cluttering up their thinking processes. Cooperation and forthright communication with others, although quite difficult now, must be pursued in order to overcome pessimism.

Here in the Libra-Capricorn square, loyalties are divided between the partner at home and partners at work. Both place heavy demands upon these natives, and they have a choice to make about the relative importance of these partners in their daily life.

Transiting Pluto in Libra Opposite Natal Mercury in Aries

Mercury in Aries expresses its ideas powerfully, immediately and often with disregard for others' responses. Individuals going through this aspect are engrossed in their own ideas, thoughts and plans, listening to no one. They usually jump into instantaneous action, hammering away at the nails of their project even before others are aware of the fact that the lumber has arrived.

No one can go it alone all the time, since our daily lives are made up of constant interaction with others. In order to achieve their ambitious Arian goals they must learn to cooperate with others. Before they pass their final examination in this difficult lesson, they will probably have knocked not only their own heads against a wall, but the unwilling heads of many others in the process.

Transiting Pluto in Libra Conjunct Natal Venus in Libra

The highest attribute of this aspect encourages close encounters of the finest kind. One may now attract another who will be a lifelong love or one with whom there will be a brief but passionate love affair. Love knows no halfway measures here.

A Pluto-Venus conjunction can also bring about the death or final parting of a beloved, as Pluto clears away what is no longer needed for the natives' growth and paves the way for a new, more stable and satisfying relationship.

Their finely-tempered sense of beauty finds expression in their home and surroundings with the acquisition of art objects or luxurious personal items. Creativity is also released in using what potential skills they may have in painting, writing and music.

Transiting Pluto in Libra
Trine Natal Venus in Gemini

The Geminian social butterfly flutters forth here to flit happily from one party to another. Sparkling gaily, these individuals enjoy meeting new people and drawing them out in friendly conversation. Completely at ease, their popularity soars as they wander happily from buffet table to barbecue grill making new friends along the way.

This transit is an excellent time to take short trips which will probably result in several interesting friendships.

Transiting Pluto in Libra
Trine Natal Venus in Aquarius

The natives' social life will increase now, for as they radiate charm and happy feelings, others wish to share their company. They accept new acquaintances easily at their worth and on their level, drawing them out in conversation about work and hobbies. Now is an excellent time to join business organizations, social clubs, and other group activities.

Transiting Pluto in Libra
Square Natal Venus in Cancer

This transit brings into the life a period of forced self-evaluation. The native's insecurity surfaces and they suffer feelings of rejection, unworthiness and disappointment. Circumstances, possibly the end of an intense love affair, now cause them to draw into themselves, nursing their wounds and wondering if they will ever be able to love again. Overcoming the pain of the experience and relegating it to its proper niche in their memories is vital, for again Pluto is getting rid of what is no longer needed.

If the relationship was fraught with jealousy, selfish demands and unhealthy dependence, then with Pluto's purging, these individuals will eventually realize they are better and stronger without it. Living alone for awhile will help them overcome misery and straighten out their tangled emotions.

All of this may have been brought about by the natives' subtle manipulation of others to fulfill their own desires. Loved ones may rebel, may walk away from too much mothering or smothering care. Their natural impulse is to escape the suffocating bonds of a union founded on emotional captivity.

Transiting Pluto in Libra Square Natal Venus in Capricorn

Venusian people, concerned with prestige and stability, may find themselves in an emotional war brought on by a fierce sexual attraction to someone not on their social level. Struggling with strong Plutonian love urges, they crash headlong into their Capricorn conservatism, for it is inbred in them to look for a partner who fits well into their scheme of business and financial success and place in the community. When this transit hits, a man may get involved with a woman of limited education and no refinement, while a woman, whose appearance is the epitome of society's lady, may have a furtive, but turbulent affair with the guy at the car wash.

Sooner or later, Pluto forces the individual to see the situation in its true light, and in so doing common sense takes over again.

Transiting Pluto in Libra Opposing Natal Venus in Aries

Venus in Aries flames brightly for here it inherits some of the Martian characteristics. Its expression is ardent, outgoing, aggressive. These natives know what they want in love affairs and usually boldly pursue the one to whom they are most strongly attracted. Here Venus bucks up against the holding action of Pluto, which seeks to slow things down, to give individuals the chance to consider seriously if this is what they truly desire in their love life, now and forevermore. Libra wants its mate for a long-term commitment whereas Venus in Aries may experience a deeply moving love experience tonight and be gone in the morning.

The Libran qualities of intelligence, good taste and fine social manners are considerably ruffled by the aggression of Venus in Aries. Since Aries and Libra are often carrying on an uneasy peace, which occasionally disrupts into open warfare, the native's predicament in handling these divergent energies is fraught with difficulties. During this transit, the Plutonian experience will dampen the Venusian ardor as a result of some painful emotional affair so that it will eventually merge in harmony with the delicate Venusian qualities of Libra.

Transiting Pluto in Libra Conjunct Natal Mars in Libra

This dynamic aspect can best be used by putting affairs in order, for now personal energy is running at an all-time high. Properly channeled, they can wield it to seek promotions in career, work out business partnerships and affairs and take constructive action in their personal life.

Their vibrant self-expression will be well received by those close to them and their courage to be their own self arouses admiration. This can be a time of great achievement if the individuals harness their passions and energies into productive enterprises with helpmates and partners.

Transiting Pluto in Libra Trine Natal Mars in Gemini

Many original ideas spark the life now and these individuals waste no time in putting them into action. They eagerly dismiss outworn attitudes and notions from daily routine, while at the same time inaugurating new methods of communication in their chosen work. It is an excellent period for teaching, public speaking, taking short jurneys and answering correspondence from their many friends. Here the two air signs compliment each other well.

Transiting Pluto in Libra Trine Natal Mars in Aquarius

The Aquarian flair for invention is stimulated during this transit. Individuals may now profit from any ideas they can transform into concrete and practical realities.

They may enjoy working with young children in scouting and little league activities, or volunteer in community affairs to work for better playgrounds and parks. They are happy organizing competitive sports in group events. In true Aquarian fashion they are open, eager and friendly to everyone who crosses their path as they welcome them into their brotherhood of action.

Transiting Pluto in Libra Square Natal Mars in Cancer

Arguments and squabbles in the family circle erupt at this time. Cancerian people constantly feel slighted, overlooked, rejected and retire into their shell dragging hurt feelings with them. They may use sex as a weapon during this period by either demanding too much from the partner or withholding it as punishment for bad behavior.

Anything that has bothered the native from childhood should be hauled out, examined and acted upon to relieve inner tensions. Mars is often uncomfortable in the sign of Cancer, using its energies to express negative emotions rather than putting them into beneficial physical activities.

Transiting Pluto in Libra Square Natal Mars in Capricorn

Power struggles arise at work for the native. They feel tensions building around them even as they are working hard to achieve success. This may cause them to overwork, sacrificing and exhausting their well-known efficiency. Tempers may flare out of control as frustrations mount inside. The solution lies not in being openly aggressive, but in attempting to integrate some of the Libran qualities of cooperation and fair play, not only in the market place, but also at home.

Transiting Pluto in Libra Opposite Natal Mars in Aries

Here the energies of Mars, ruling its own sign, can be overwhelming. It is imperative that the natives' review their behavior in order to determine if they are so overly concerned about their own desires that they cannot see another's point of view. Their energy is either overstimulated in answering to their strong will by riding callously over everyone or, conversely, it is wasted away in a succession of unbearable frustrations. They are frequently at cross purposes in career demands and close relationships.

Until they learn to be objective about life's circumstances, they will compound their dilemmas with their impatient, impulsive nature. Life becomes a boxing ring where they fight an endless battle with a sparring partner. The partners may keep changing, but they do not. The inner-self, which tries to surface during the transit, will in time break through and show them the way to bring about renewal by holding the undesirable qualities of their nature under control.

Transiting Pluto in Libra Conjunct Natal Jupiter in Libra

A deeper understanding of all ninth house matters is felt by the Jupiter-in-Libra natives as they examine and absorb religious concepts and philosophical learnings. They are now able to put this knowledge to use in a positive way, which brings out leadership qualities and inspires those around them. Faith and optimism are boundless now as they make extensive plans which have an excellent chance of success under this transit.

Transiting Pluto in Libra Trine Natal Jupiter in Gemini

Whatever is studied now can be put to practical use. An abundance of intellectual harmony and curiosity makes itself felt, enabling the natives to write seriously on subjects of marriage, love affairs, social problems and psychological studies. Geminis prepare themselves by thoroughly researching their topic before they present it to their peers.

Transiting Pluto in Libra Trine Natal Jupiter in Aquarius

Many subjects expand the natives' knowledge at this time. They are particularly interested in political activities, group participation in government reform, new religious creeds and anything touching upon futuristic concepts which will help humankind. Their broad range vision encompasses democratic ideals brought into proper perspective where they will aid the average citizen. Optimism radiates from them as they stand on busy street corners collecting signatures from passers-by for issues like tax reform legislation.

Transiting Pluto in Libra Square Jupiter in Cancer

Natives under this transit may become fanatics about a new religion which they feel is the answer to all our difficulties. They bear down hard on family and friends, trying to convert them to their unorthodox beliefs. These tactics may result in estrangement from loved ones who refuse to put up with this dictatorial approach but, nevertheless, love them and are concerned about their strange behavior.

At this time individuals need to detach themselves from this preoccupation and take a long view of the problem. Pluto will help them to decide what is worthwhile in their concepts and what needs to be thrown out. In time, their loving Cancerian nature will be restored to its normal function of outgoing affection.

Transiting Pluto in Libra Square Jupiter in Capricorn

The overabundance of Jupiter expresses itself in the Capricorn concern for business and career advancements to the detriment of close relationships and understanding of others. Workaholics surface here, those who spend their time and energies consumed by the demands of the piles of papers on their desk. They can be so driven by their desire for success that, under the challenging aspects of the transit, they may resort to dishonesty, subterfuge or wheeling and dealing–actions they would not ordinarily consider. But, the power struggle within must be dealt with, one way or the other, and their principles in public and private life will be put to the Plutonian test.

Transiting Pluto in Libra Opposing Natal Jupiter in Aries

Here individuals take on too much, expect too much, and try too hard. Their optimism runs away with them. They are guilty of overdoing, starting projects with insufficient financial backing, forcing religious ideas on their followers, expounding on strange cults and creeds. They may be swept away by some weird religion as they follow the guru or the pied piper down a mystical path. They chant their new-found beliefs to all who will listen and try to convert them with Aries enthusiasm.

Their impractical plans and strange behavior sooner or later will backfire. Then they will be faced with the urgency to straighten out their real needs from the false ones and to look at life realistically. They may find this a difficult task, but once Pluto separates the wheat from the chaff, they will be able to use the Jupiterian forces for ultimate good.

Transiting Pluto in Libra
Conjunct Natal Saturn in Libra

Here the Pluto transforming forces allied with the Saturnian stability herald a new dimension in arriving at positive long-range goals. The Saturn-in-Libra natives, with their strong will-power and desire for self-improvement, may change careers at this time as their concerns are awakened to more practical and secure measures in life. They work long and hard to realize their ambitions, accepting responsibilities, using patience and resourcefulness to structure their daily life and win plaudits in their career.

Transiting Pluto in Libra
Trine Natal Saturn in Gemini

The natives now experience ease in writing on serious subjects, compiling texts and information after careful research. Their usual Geminian frivolity has been subdued while their natural curiosity, interest in vocabulary and sentence structure take on a reflective tone. At this time, they can tackle two jobs and do them equally well, for their concentration is finely focused and their energies well-directed.

Transiting Pluto in Libra
Trine Natal Saturn in Aquarius

During this transit, individuals may become interested in politics and national concerns. The Saturnian influence can find expression in projects involving preservation of natural resources and solutions to present day problems of energy and water conservation. Their excellent organizational abilities are stimulated to restructure and reform existing conditions within the power bases.

Transiting Pluto in Libra Square Natal Saturn in Cancer

This transit can be most beneficial to individuals because it causes them to rely upon themselves in order to attain their goals. If they have been leaning upon others or expecting help, they will be brought up short. They will discover that they may be only interested in helping themselves and creating their own power base. Ultimately, they will realize they have greater strength within themselves than they had thought possible, as they tackle one by one, all the obstacles, frustrations, restrictions and rejections blocking their path of progress. They must learn to use the Saturnian patience, persistence and fortitude to propel them out of this dark period.

From the past, some overlooked responsibilities may catch up to them, taking up much of their time needlessly. They will experience strong desires to be alone, to hole up in a corner with their miseries. This is one of the most difficult transits to grapple with, for many times they will feel a kind of hopeless desperation. When it is all behind they will climb out of their personal darkness to discover they have survived the slings and arrows, that life does go on, and they have a far deeper understanding of its meaning than ever before.

Transiting Pluto in Libra Square Natal Saturn in Capricorn

Saturn in its own sign is extremely strong, but here it is thrown into a hard cardinal square with Libra. Whatever is attempted during this period may end in frustration for timing, in some inexplicable way, is off. Individuals may take too much responsibility which is not really theirs, and thus antagonize others. They may put in long hours at work which may end in lack of achievement. It is possible they may get so tangled up in time-consuming legal affairs for a client or friend that their own work will suffer as a consequence.

With heavy pressure on them there is always the danger that they may turn to corrupt methods to attain their ends, or they may employ outright dishonesty in business affairs. Conversely, they may discover corruption in their own office, but through other pressures, be kept from bringing it out in the open. Since Saturn is so powerful here, and with Pluto equally as powerful, these souls must wait with patience and fortitude for the negative forces to surface in their lives so that they can face them and eliminate them forever.

Transiting Pluto in Libra Opposing Saturn in Aries

Slow-moving Saturn in this position delays the fencing and swordplay that goes on between Aries and Libra. The contest here is in earnest as Libra, strengthened by Pluto, plays a subtle withholding game, while Aries' natural urge for action is hindered by Saturn's presence. All four elements are here: Pluto's water, Libra's air, Saturn's earth and Aries' fire, contributing on one hand to balance, and on the other to a stalemate.

The Saturn-in-Aries person, undergoing the stabilizing effect of Saturn, must be taught the vital need for interplay, for mutual give and take, a shaking of hands across the border lines with the Libran Pluto. Two possible outcomes are apparent: harmony as the two halves meet and become one, or destruction as the powerful energies knock each other out of the game forever. These individuals are forced to deal with the challenge, to parcel out the elements, some air here for intellect, a bucket of earth there for practicality, a few drops of water for feeling, a flickering flame for action. In time, they will experience emotional and mental harmony, instead of torture on the rack. After great anguish comes great achievement, and it is all possible in this powerhouse aspect.

Transiting Pluto in Libra Trine Uranus in Gemini

Uranus in Gemini: August 8, 1941, to October 5, 1941; May 15, 1942, to August 30, 1948; November 13, 1948, to June 10, 1949.

This is the time to do the unexpected and Gemini does it well. Charisma radiates as these individuals fall happily into the arms of Pluto in Libra. Whatever events come hurtling into their lives they are ready for and accept them eagerly. Great mental stimulation occurs. They are aroused to consider another's viewpoint, explore thoroughly what previously had manifested as idle curiosity, research a subject earnestly as they broaden the scope of their intellect. The Geminian talents combine easily with the Libran charm as they bustle about, redecorating their surroundings in bright, happy colors, throwing impromptu parties for all their new friends, playing matchmaker for the shy ones. They are at their all-time best as they roll with the Uranian punches and get up from the floor with not a hair out of place.

Transiting Pluto in Libra Trine Natal Uranus in Aquarius

Uranus in Aquarius: January 31, 1912, to September 4, 1912; November 12, 1912, to March 31, 1919; August 17, 1919, to January 21, 1920.

Two air signs, blending together in harmonious aspect, bring many rewards for the natives' intellectual ambitions. It is indeed a happy time as Uranus, strong in its own sign, opens up doors to exciting adventures: places to go, things to do, people to meet and new ideas to conceptualize. Now individuals can break away easily from dreary life styles and stuffy situations to embrace a new realm of activity as they change into new clothes, wear a new hair style, welcome new friends and acquaintances into their charmed circle. Someone (a beautiful stranger perhaps) will invade their private Aquarian space, shaking them up to the excitement of living, loving and sharing in their revitalized social structure.

Transiting Pluto in Libra Square Uranus in Cancer

Uranus in Cancer: August 31, 1948, to November 12, 1948; June 11, 1949, to August 24, 1955; January 29, 1956, to June 9, 1956.

Here we have a generation that wants freedom in their lives. They may now experience a compulsion to break away from home and strike out on their own as they reach their early twenties. Perhaps they may travel a long distance from their birthplace, breaking family ties completely to settle in a new environment. Or they may acquire their own apartment in the same community, thereby registering independence, but keeping in touch. Facing the world alone and paying their own bills is not easy but they are among the millions of young people who have chosen this route to the alternate one of staying home, as previous generations did, and being dominated and controlled by parents.

With their new-found intoxicating liberties, these natives may literally break the Cancerian laws of marriage and family by living with a person without legal sanction, or drifting indiscriminately from one sexual partner to another or experimenting with homosexuality as an alternative life-style. If the native is a woman she may bear a child out of wedlock, openly and happily without fear of moral censure. Or the native, man or woman, may break the strongest Cancerian bond of all, in their outspoken intent to be childless in order to pursue their goals unhampered by financial sacrifices and emotional responsibilities.

All of this goes against the Cancerian grain. Mothers and fathers from an older generation stand by, sadly shaking their heads, wondering how it can happen to their children, when they have given them the best years of their lives, educated them and shown them which path to follow for emotional satisfaction.

As these natives, along with their generation, blast their trumpets in the clarion call to freedom, they may hear dissonant music from the Pluto orchestra and the Libran musicians who are asking, "How can you have emotional security and freedom at the same time? You must realize you cannot have it both ways." Thus they must learn the art of compromise, for emotional security demands a giving, a loving, a sharing with other people in their lives. Without this, their lives may become shallow and meaningless, even as they look at their beautiful homes with no one else in them and the plaques of achievement hanging on the walls.

Transiting Pluto in Libra Opposing Uranus in Aries

Uranus in Aries: March 31, 1927, to November 4, 1927; January 13, 1928, to June 6, 1934; October 11, 1934, to March 27, 1935.

This aspect is one of the most powerful and difficult to handle. It is a final confrontation between opposing forces—the old and the new, the familiar and the strange, the needed and the unneccessary—as they face each other on either side of the Plutonian stream bubbling up from the subconscious. Will one side burn the bridge that crosses the stream? Or will the energies lay down their arms, walk toward each other and meet in the middle of the bridge? Will these Uranus-in-Aries natives willingly accept the end of the old regime and the beginning of the new, or will they be forced by some severe emotional crisis to rebuild the bridge from the stones left lying around after the explosion?

Exciting challenges are hurled at them from all directions in their personal and private lives. If they refuse to take on these challenges (which is highly unlike the Aries personality), they will be strung out in a ceaseless battle between what they were and what they may become. In seeking freedom they may carry it to extremes and alienate those around them in their freewheeling independence. They must get rid of their resentments, the emotional baggage of self-defeating patterns in the past, sweeping it away through the Plutonian forces of renewal, in exchange for a fresh start with a new perspective and a greater understanding of the value of closeness with others in the life experience.

The message of these powerful energies, which are fighting for the control of the native, is saying in effect, "You are entitled to your freedom, but only when you learn to control it and pay respect to other people in your world."

Transiting Pluto in Libra Sextile Natal Neptune in Leo

Neptune in Leo: September 23, 1914, to December 14, 1914; July 19, 1915, to March 19, 1916; May 2, 1916, to September 20, 1928; February 20, 1929, to July 23, 1929.

The subtlety of Pluto and the illusionary influence of Neptune come together here in an aspect of opportunity. Individuals will feel an interest in spiritual matters, be drawn to meditation and the development of higher intuition.

Neptune in Leo deals with the natives' sense of identity. Here they may imagine themselves to be king in their own restricted world. Pluto urges them to tune themselves in to a more realistic level. Now is the time to listen to what others are saying, particularly those who are close and with whom they may be having problems in relationships. After analyzing it and taking the best of advice, they may find their life circumstances improving. Neptune's rose-colored glasses must be removed, for here Pluto gives the chance to confront their environment on a more realistic level.

Since it is a sextile aspect, the two energies can work well together, complimenting the finer qualities of each.

Transiting Pluto in Libra Conjunct Natal Neptune in Libra

Neptune in Libra: October 4, 1942, to April 18, 1943; August 3, 1943, to December 23, 1955; March 12, 1956, to October 18, 1956; June 17, 1957, to August 4, 1957.

The children who were born during World War II and the post-war baby boom, are now in their early twenties to late thirties, and are presently experiencing the conjunction of Pluto to their natal Neptune. During this fifteen year transit, an entire generation is undergoing the dynamic impact of one heavy planet blending its force with another. These powerful energies combine the water element of Neptune, ruler of Pisces, and Pluto, ruler of Scorpio, with the fire of Leo and the air of Libra. Thus, as Pluto enters Libra to transit the natal Neptune positions, the intellectuality of the seventh house ruler becomes vitally important.

In the natal sextile position transiting Pluto conjunct natal Neptune evidences an idealistic concern with love affairs and close relationships. These natives are fraught with an emotional intensity, looking upon the loved one as a figure of perfection, embodying the utmost in beauty, character, loyalty and devotion. Here is the one who will take them by the hand and lead them to their personal Utopia, sharing a closeness and understanding which is the life blood of Libra. Happily, they bow down to their vision of radiance atop the Neptunian pedestal. Such idealism is impractical, unworkable, unreal in today's jittery world. As Pluto slowly rolls along through Libra, it goes to work unveiling the mystery surrounding the beloved, exposing the god or goddess as an average human being blemished with irritating mannerisms and annoying personality defects. Often this period of disenchantment represents a drastic and painful experience to the native as he or she grapples with the tattered remnants of a love affair. They do not want their illusions shattered, but Pluto forces them to analyze the bond with a clear rational mind in the harsh light of day.

If one is able to accept the tearing away of the veil of mystery and the toppling from the pedestal, then the loved one will be clearly seen in a realistic manner which will be mutually beneficial to the relationship. Quite often the two people involved, if close in age, will be going through the change and upheaval at approximately the same time. In that case they may be able to recognize what is happening, accept it eagerly and build anew from the ashes of the old.

One result of this head-on assault with realism has manifested in the widely accepted practice of a couple living together in all the aspects and trappings of a marriage, but without benefit of a legal ceremony. Millions of young people choose to work out their involvements in this manner. They decide to find out first if their love attraction would hold up and work well on a daily basis with the glamour stripped away. They may be mindful of their parents (the Pluto-in-Cancer generation) who were raised on romance and spoon fed on role-playing of the big, masterful husband and the meek, helpful, obedient wife. They may have observed how often this concept no longer works in today's world where the rights of women as individuals have become increasingly important and all pervasive. So they choose to pool their furniture and groceries, splitting the rent, foregoing raising a family, just to see if the gears mesh. And if they do not, if disillusionment rears its head, if fighting and bickering over money and sex take over, then they are able to move away with no great harm done, no lifelong scars inflicted, calling an end to the experiment in true Plutonian fashion.

In all of this, the intellectual quality of the air sign, Libra, surges to the fore and its influence is strongly felt. The final result of the Plutonian transit is the acceptance of the importance of each person's intellectual qualities in the success of a relationship. These young people view each other dispassionately, analyzing their situation without rancor. They have achieved a meeting of the minds on the same level, which, they discover, is equally as important as the physical attraction. Leo wants each person to maintain his or her unique personality, whereas Libra needs a responsive partner who is also operating from an equal base. Pluto extends a hand in sextile from Leo to Libra saying, "Come with me; we will enjoy life and share it together."

If the native is unable to accept or even understand the Plutonian urge to strip away the mystery from love affairs, then deep psychological problems may surface. Negative Neptunian influences can cause chaotic conditions. The native, trying to hang on stubbornly to dreams of perfection, may drift away from reality into an involvement with one who finds escape from the harshness of living into a world of alcohol or drugs. Then, at the expense of their own self-worth and mental health, they may put up with the degrading, pitiful demands of the loved one, for their Leo pride wants to be needed and their Libran qualities find fulfillment only with a partner, no matter how disturbing or self-defeating that person can be. The native chooses to be a martyr, hanging on to their dependency in a most negative way. The obsessions of Pluto and the delusions of Neptune exert their forces in the destruction of two people feeding on each other's unhealthy compulsions.

It has already been mentioned elsewhere that Pluto, stripping away the Neptunian veil, has called our attention to the condition of women, the black race and other minorities in the Libran search for equality. Pluto now forces us to look at the manner in which we have been indoctrinated for generations to regiment certain groups, plugging them into various boxes and pigeonholes for our own convenience. Now we must consider them as whole human beings with talents and abilities to contribute to the well-being of the world.

Many changes are being made for the millions touched by this transit. Let it be known that whatever Pluto changes, such changes are forevermore irrevocable.

Transiting Pluto in Libra Square Natal Pluto in Cancer

Pluto in Cancer: September 24, 1912, to October 2, 1912; July 12, 1913, to December 25, 1913; May 23, 1914, to October 8, 1937; November 15, 1937, to August 5, 1938; February 7, 1939, to June 15, 1939.

The people born with Pluto in Cancer must now assimilate the meaning of Pluto in a sign square to its natal position. This transit is now affecting individuals born in the time span mentioned above; people who are at an age where they are well-established with home, family, career and roots in the community.

These natives, whether men or women, have been raised in an era which clearly defined male and female roles. The man was head of the family, handling the money, making the important decisions, laying down the rules of behavior for his wife and children to follow. The woman was dependent, subservient, carrying on in an unflagging effort to please as she ignored or repressed her own desires and needs. Now Libra shakes up this concept with its emphasis on equality and fairness, while Pluto extorts the individual to discard from his or her life attitudes and beliefs which no longer are working or have value in today's changing world. It was not by chance that the women's liberation movement gained strength and stature when Pluto entered Libra in 1971.

Taking the sexes individually, the female native

is experiencing the greater change in her life. In many cases she has had the courage to shuck off a stale and stunted marriage for the freedom to be herself, seeking the opportunity to use her long-neglected talents in creativity which go beyond the bonds of the rolling pin and mom's apple pie.

The male native runs headlong into the changes happening all around him as the female discovers new strength and dignity in being a woman. He finds that he is no longer accepted enthusiastically in any life situation simply because he is a man with all the prerogatives of superiority. He must now meet the female on an equal level, not only in marriage, but also in business and social life.

If a man and woman in a marriage were born within a few years of each other they will experience the effects of this transit at the same time.

Notwithstanding the stress that is created, a note of optimism creeps through. If the marriage has been a solid one, built on mutual respect, understanding and mature love it can go forward to a new dimension where the couple may inaugurate satisfying changes in their lives. They may decide to pull up their stakes and move to another state or country, use their resources and savings in starting a jointly run business, or merely enjoy the release from family responsibilities. They may decide to travel to faraway places, buy a different type of home, take courses together at a higher academic level or indulge a mutual interest in a hobby. In a solid marriage, it can even manifest in the rarest of events: a second honeymoon!

Transiting Pluto in Libra Sextile Natal Pluto in Leo

The generation born with Pluto in Leo, which thrust itself upon the world's consciousness during the turbulent 1960's, is now coming of age as Pluto sends its sextile from Libra, the sign of balance, to the natal placement of Pluto in Leo. These young people who became vocal concerning government policies, protested the Viet Nam war, burned their draft cards and shouted outrageous demands from college campuses, have now settled down peacefully and are in the process of becoming part of a reformed establishment they have helped create.

It is interesting to observe how the Uranus-Pluto transit through Virgo in the 1960's brought out all the Leo characteristics in this generation. The Leo egotism demanded immediate change as they dramatized their protests with violence and hysteria. They wanted it all right away; they simply could not wait.

Now with Libra sending its soothing influence to their natal charts, the calming effect of the sign of balance and harmony takes over. These natives have realized that the most effective way to accomplish their ends (many of which were necessary and vitally important) is through the proper channels in a court of law. They are learning the impact of equality and fairness in all its Libran force as they work industriously with fierce energy to accomplish their commendable aims. They willingly share their talents in partnerships with others, working for a common cause in rooting out many of the inequities in modern life. Many are pledged toward helping minorities achieve a better education and a fair share of the job market. They have at long last melted into a positive mainstream of American life.

Since this generation is still young, they learn and adapt easily. The double dose of Pluto is a stepping stone of great strength and meaning as it offers not only opportunity, but the tangible rewards of energies wisely used. The two signs are proclaiming, "Let us have equality among kings, for each one of us is a king. Let us share the limelight on the world's stage for we can all bask in our individual ray of light." Libra and Leo are basically a mutual admiration society and here it comes to full bloom as the powerful Leo energy and the Libran checks and balances merge with the finest of the Plutonian powers.

BOOK THREE

PLUTO AND THE FUTURE

CHAPTER NINE

TRANSITING PLUTO INSIDE THE ORBIT OF NEPTUNE 1978-2000

Humankind today is confronted with an extraordinary situation as it looks first on the one hand at abundance and on the other at starvation; at governments founded on freedom and individual rights, and those ruled by tyranny and terror; at great learning and education and at illiteracy and ignorance; at glowing health and at the spreading of illness and disease; at greater attempts at equality in law and at rampant crime. The world is full of woe and it seems to the average citizen, as they plug along in their daily grind, that it increases at an alarming rate every day.

It would seem at first hand that the position of two planets in the galaxy could not have any bearing or even a solution to our world-wide dilemmas. But astrology in its unfathomable wisdom, has seen fit to bring about the alignment of two intense planets in sextile aspect: Pluto in Libra and Neptune in Sagittarius. This aspect, starting in 1940 as Pluto accelerated its speed to catch up to Neptune, will last to the year 2000.

Stephen Arroyo in his text, *Astrology, Karma and Transformation,* has described this phenomenon thusly:

> "The orbit of Pluto, like the orbits of all other planets, is an ellipse, but Pluto's orbit is considerably more elliptical than that of any other major planet in the solar system . . . Pluto is now approaching the perihelion point in its orbit, or that closest to the Sun; but it will not pass that point until the year 1989, when it will be at a distance from the Sun only slightly less than that of Neptune (2,800,000,000 miles). Pluto will then be nearest to the Earth as well as to the Sun and in the most favorable position generally for observation from the Earth.
>
> It is an interesting circumstance that if its orbit lay in the same plane as that of the orbit of Neptune, Pluto at perihelion would be slightly within the orbit of Neptune. As a result of the high mutual inclination of the orbital planes of the two planets, however, their orbits do not intersect at any point, although at its closest approach to the Sun, Pluto is actually a bit (approximately half an astronomical unit) nearer to the Sun than is Neptune. According to Dr. Franklin of the Hayden Planetarium in New York City, Pluto will move closer to the Sun in its orbit than Neptune on December 11, 1978 and will remain there until March 14, 1999."[14]

A sextile aspect is one of opportunity, so from an astrological point of view, here is our opportunity to blend the energies flowing from these planets using their strongest attributes: the wisdom of Sagittarius, the compassion of Neptune, the equality and fairness of Libra and the regeneration of Pluto. Lasting peace in the world is possible if we open our hearts in understanding of others, use the wisdom of the academic and scientific communities to solve our dilemmas and, from the depths of our murky past, to purge our individual souls of the hypocrisy and greed which have assailed us from the beginning of time.

The basic meaning of Pluto has been thoroughly delineated in this book. Now let us consider Neptune whose meaning in traditional astrology has been mainly one of formlessness and negativity. In book after book, we have encountered the astrological jargon depicting its deceitful, dissolving, illusory nature. Little has been written about its transcending force. Our belief is that the planet of the mists sends out vibrations of great hope for humankind, for as the ruler of Pisces, it opens up the door to the global twelfth house and lets in its radiant light.

Still in sextile aspect, Pluto moves into Scorpio in 1983, and Neptune into Capricorn in 1984, adding other dimensions to their powers. With the Capricorn-Saturn influence, a structure of world government could be built on a firm foundation with all the nations of the world contributing their share to its success on a practical level. With the Scorpio qualities we are given the inspiration to understand those who are different from us. As all of these vibrations flow toward us from the outer-reaches of the galaxy, not only to you and me, but to the billions inhabiting this planet, maybe now, at last, will we find our way to that longed-for Utopia, our peace on earth forevermore. It is indeed our last chance, for if we do not handle these powerhouse energies properly, the deep side of Pluto will erupt in a cataclysmic upheaval which may possibly wipe us off the face of the earth.

In its twentieth century journey Neptune, first in Cancer, gave us an idealistic concern with home and family; in Leo it flavored and buttressed the ego and the individuality; in Virgo it highlighted the practical ideal in service and health; in Libra it brought the desire for closeness with others; and in Scorpio the compulsion to search inward and ask, "Who are we?" Now in its transit through Sagittarius it questions, "Who are they?"

"They" are the rest of the world, teeming billions overseas in other countries, following strange religions, unpopular governmental concepts, bizarre standards of living, unusual marriage and sexual customs. With few exceptions we, here in the United States, have previously not been able (or, indeed, cared) to try to understand them. Throughout the ages philosophers have asked, "What manner of man is this?" when a foreigner appeared in the market place, ready to barter spices and silks for the local corn and tobacco. Their religion was incomprehensible to the western world, their speech a mixture of strange sounds, their money a fistful of rare coins. But they had come a long way to arrive on our shores, to study our equally odd conduct, our curious liberties, and to take home fascinating tales of our peculiar behavior.

When Uranus was discovered in the 19th century its qualities in time became associated with freedom of thought and scientific advancement. Many inventions came forth—the wireless, the telephone, the automobile, the airplane, motion pictures, radio, television. The world aroused itself and got in touch with its neighbors. Now, in the latter half of the twentieth century, any one of us can step on a plane and in less than 24 hours be in China, Japan, Kenya, Argentina, New South Wales. We can communicate in minutes to any living soul within reasonable distance of a telephone. We can bounce photographs of the day's news off international satellites; and, we can put a man (and soon, perhaps a woman!) on the moon.

With all of this hardware at our disposal, we can ask ourselves: "What are we doing with it to foster international understanding, to know each other better?" Or are we going to continue to broadcast only the screaming headlines of catastrophes and disagreements leaving the heartwarming news about the little people doing the good and decent thing buried on the inside pages?

So how do we learn about others in order to see them as individuals? Such comprehension does not come about by leaping aboard supersonic jets, not by checking in at the international Hiltons, not by staying in our own little clannish group as we travel. It is by traveling leisurely through a country, on bicycles as college students have done, and by staying in hostels, by rubbing elbows in the market place, breaking bread with a family in their home, listening to the local gossip. In the struggle to know another's daily life we can then begin to understand the other person underneath the different skin and the strange dress and the peculiar customs. As we get to know them, we will discover that they, too, as well as their families, experience their moments of happiness and sorrow, success and failure, birth and death.

These sophisticated methods of communication brought us an event we had not considered or bargained for, a close-up of the Viet Nam war on our living room television screens. War has always been with us, inescapably, as we turn back the rumpled pages of history to review its horrifying clashes, its brutal battles in the name of religion, its greedy grasping for other lands and resources. But it was always something most of us had read about, not something we watched with a feeling of repulsion and helplessness, as men were slaughtered before our eyes every night on the evening news.

For centuries it was thought that peace for humankind was an impossible goal. Most of the world's leaders led us to believe that war was the only way to solve our differences. Why then don't we forget about peace and succumb to the savagery which is alleged to be basic in our nature? The people of the world have listened to this siren song through the ages and bowed their heads to its inevitability. It has been only recently during the

Viet Nam conflict when its validity was questioned. The questions were raised by the vibrant generation of Pluto-in-Leo young people who, with typical faith in their own identities, refused to bargain their future and be swept into a hopeless, inhuman, stalemated war.

Can the living justify the war to any young man who has died in the service of his country? Indeed, he cannot hear your prayers or see your tears. Can we raise him from the dead and ask him: "Was it worth it to lose your life this way?" How can we ever know, without rationalizing the fact that we who are still living must assume this to be true. If this unknown soldier answered otherwise he would be considered un-American, un-Russian, un-Japanese. Look around at all the young men who have openly stated they will not fight for their country in a war of aggression on another's soil. Consider the countless married couples who choose not to have children for they are unwilling to raise them to adulthood only to have them become the target of the enemy. The youth back in the 1960's may have had the right idea when they shouted, "Make love - not war!"

So we reach a point where we ask ourselves: "Is there not a better way? Must we go eternally onward ripping our mutual earth apart at stated intervals, polluting its air and water and soil with nuclear garbage, maiming and killing its youth to satisfy the ego demands of corrupt governments and their aged leaders? What does it prove in the end? That one side had more hardware and ammunition than another? Has not the carnage of two World Wars, the tragedy of the Korean conflict and the senseless bloodletting of the Viet Nam massacre, has not all that been enough in one lifetime? Or is Armageddon around the corner?"

Now we must turn to Neptune for inspiration. Now we must ask Pluto, "What is good and what is evil?" Now we must depend on the wisdom of Sagittarius and the balanced scales of Libra to transcend our materialism and with Capricorn structure build us a better world in which to live.

Neptune as the ruler of Pisces means a search for true compassion. Neptune in the natural ninth house of Sagittarius expresses the ability to talk with those from other lands but on a common level about everyday affairs. Pluto in Libra's natural seventh house manifests a sincere interest in other people. The abundance of vibrations formed by these two planets draws us to strangers to converse, to bridge the gap between our world and theirs. For once we talk, once we have enough words exchanged between us, the word "stranger" disappears.

Neptune is the ruler of the twelfth house which can transcend all earthbound qualities, to reach out for what all of life means. There are no boundaries anywhere if we understand the true concept of this planet. Pluto gives Neptune the push to swing open the door to the twelfth house, to get rid of the boogey men and the bad dreams and the unspoken horrors locked away, and show them for what they truly are.

When we learn to know others as they are, when they learn to accept us as basically decent human beings who want only to live in harmony with family, friends and neighbors, then there will come the powerful purging of the whole universe as it lays down its arms, its jealousies and greed, and opens its heart and soul to compassionate understanding and eternal peace.

Aspects to the Signs from Pluto in Libra and Neptune in Sagittarius

On a personal level, the aspects from Pluto in Libra and Neptune in Sagittarius affect the twelve signs as follows:

Sign	Pluto Aspect	Influence	Neptune Aspect	Influence
Aries	Opposition	Compromise	Trine	Ease
Taurus	Quincunx	Adjustment	Quincunx	Adjustment
Gemini	Trine	Ease	Opposition	Compromise
Cancer	Square	Stress	Quincunx	Adjustment
Leo	Sextile	Creativity	Trine	Ease
Virgo	Semi-sextile	Continuity	Square	Stress
Libra	Conjunction	Power	Sextile	Creativity
Scorpio	Semi-sextile	Continuity	Semi-sextile	Continuity
Sagittarius	Sextile	Creativity	Conjunction	Power
Capricorn	Square	Stress	Semi-sextile	Continuity
Aquarius	Trine	Ease	Sextile	Creativity
Pisces	Quincunx	Adjustment	Square	Stress

Aspects to the Signs from Pluto in Scorpio and Neptune in Capricorn

On a personal level, the aspects from Pluto in Scorpio and Neptune in Capricorn affect the twelve signs as follows:

Sign	Pluto Aspect	Influence	Neptune Aspect	Influence
Aries	Quincunx	Adjustment	Square	Stress
Taurus	Opposition	Compromise	Trine	Ease
Gemini	Quincunx	Adjustment	Quincunx	Adjustment
Cancer	Trine	Ease	Opposition	Compromise
Leo	Square	Stress	Quincunx	Adjustment
Virgo	Sextile	Creativity	Trine	Ease
Libra	Semi-sextile	Continuity	Square	Stress
Scorpio	Conjunction	Power	Sextile	Creativity
Sagittarius	Semi-sextile	Continuity	Semi-sextile	Continuity
Capricorn	Sextile	Creativity	Conjunction	Power
Aquarius	Square	Stress	Semi-sextile	Continuity
Pisces	Trine	Ease	Sextile	Creativity

CHAPTER TEN
MAJOR TRANSITS TO PLUTO: 1980-2000

Saturn in Libra Conjunct Pluto in Libra

Conjunction starts in November, 1981, with Saturn at 16 degrees of Libra and Pluto at 24 degrees of Libra. Exact conjunction within one degree in November, 1982, at 27 degrees of Libra and in June, 1983, at 28 degrees of Libra. Conjunction ends in November, 1983, with Saturn at 7 degrees of Scorpio and Pluto at 29 degrees of Libra.

On a world-wide scale, the merging of the planets of discipline and regeneration may bring about changes affecting us all in our daily lives. We will be prodded into relinquishing outmoded ideas and concepts which now stand in the way of a better society. The Libran qualities of fairness and equality will be crystallized in the success of the women's liberation movement in achieving its numerous goals in the areas of employment, legal affairs, property ownership, marriage contracts, divorce settlements, birth control and abortion, credit ratings and education. All of these aims, which had their inception with the onset of the movement in the late 1960's, will finally become a reality.

Right in step with this action, the blacks, especially those in some foreign countries where persecution now exists, will win their hard-fought battle for freedom. Here in our own country, the remains of troublesome patterns in carrying out their rights will be resolved and equality in the eyes of the law and in all other aspects of daily life will finally become a living truth. By the time Saturn leaves Libra, the laws of the land will be organized effectively to assure its citizens of this reality.

Saturn in Libra will begin the process of renewing our trust in our modes of government and its administrators. In the backlash of Watergate, subtle changes have occurred and with Saturn's influence to marshall them into proper channels we will see the end of the old guard type of politician who was guilty of accepting bribes and bowing to the demands of special interest groups. Instead, we will elect younger men and women with refreshing concepts of honesty, dependability and unselfish concern for their constituents. The diehards who have been around a long time sopping up the gravy from the gravy train will be retired from the scene. A whole new feeling of revitalization coupled with the disciplined structures necessary in government will be felt by us all.

New laws will come into effect designed to cut down on the waste in government, not only financial and manpower waste, but those in connection with our use of vital natural resources, as Pluto goes through the recycling process. To save our forests, we may inaugurate programs to eliminate the scandalous waste of paper in packaging, advertising and printing. Thousands of plastic items which intrude in our daily lives and blight the landscape may be eliminated in favor of articles which can be used over and over again. Such action may bring about the return of the glass milk bottle, the china coffee cup,the sturdy rubbish can. Strict legislation regarding water and energy consumption will affect us all.

More equitable farming methods will emerge so that our technology will produce enough food to feed the populace with surpluses available for any needy countries. At the same time safer methods of birth control will be adapted for widespread use among all peoples so that their effectiveness will keep the world's population from overrunning our teeming planet.

Average citizens will be more concerned with political issues, once they realize that one small voice on the sand dunes can be effective and help to bring about the revolt against unfair taxation and other unjust legislation, and implement new laws which will be to our advantage.

Our elderly population will be treated with the respect they deserve instead of being shunted down a dead-end street. A different climate in business and the professions will utilize the skills and abilities of our older citizens as long as they can make effective contributions in our social structures. Mandatory retirement will be a thing of the past.

With the alarming increase in crime which has taken place in the last twenty years, a long hard look at its causes and effects comes up for review. As a result, criminals may be given punishments to fit their crimes, and youthful, first-time offenders will not be thrown in with hardened convicts. Certain crimes, hitherto overlooked and purposely ignored such as rape, incest, child molesting and wife-beating will be treated with the severity they deserve.

Educational programs instigated by both government agencies and private citizens will flourish in the ghettos and slums in serious attempts to eliminate the breeding grounds of criminals. Concerned citizens will join in helping to train these youths in useful skills which can assure them a decent place in society.

On a personal level, individuals will be drawn to more stable life expressions, especially in their work as they seek security and a firm foundation. They have good concentration now, along with heightened self-discipline, which will assure success. Saturn brings a much needed sense of stability, decorum, responsibility and control into our lives.

Saturn in Capricorn Sextile Pluto in Scorpio

Sextile starts December, 1988, with Saturn at 5 degrees of Capricorn and Pluto at 13 degrees of Scorpio: exact sextile from April,

1989, to June, 1989, with Saturn at 13 degrees of Capricorn and Pluto at 14, 13, 12 degrees of Scorpio: Exact sextile from December, 1989, to January, 1990, with Saturn at 15, 16 degrees of Capricorn and Pluto at 16, 17 degrees of Scorpio: Sextile ends in January 1991 with Saturn at 27 degrees of Capricorn and Pluto at 19 degrees of Scorpio.

Here both planets in their own signs bring a powerhouse combination to world affairs and to our own lives. Fortunately, the signs they inhabit are sextile to each other so the energies flow freely.

Uranus, preceding Pluto through Scorpio, blasted the door open to the secrets and scandals involving the use of other people's money in insurance frauds, unsafe banking practices, unfair taxation and other unsavory operations. It also marked the period when inflation soared and, as a result, reduced the buying power of each individual.

Now, Pluto in its own sign, can clear up these questionable procedures. Saturn stands firm, giving the people the backbone to pursue these necessary changes through the proper governmental channels. It will be, in effect, the taxpayers' bloodless revolution on paper, accomplished legally by men and women sitting amicably around a table, throwing out the red tape, the ambiguous old laws and passing new legislation to protect individuals and their money. Many government workers who have mooched along in soft jobs for years may find themselves out on the street, unemployed, as

Saturn and Pluto consolidate, organize, and sweep out the dross.

The importance of this transit can best be understood by taking the strength of these two positions and using them to one's advantage. It is a time when strong moral codes will again be popular and one's sense of responsibility comes back in favor. The days of expecting the government to solve every problem which befell the average person—to find jobs, to pay the unemployed, to reimburse medical bills, to lend money for a new house, a new business, more education—all of these, along with the taxes to foot the expense, have been somewhat overdone. Now the pendulum swings back to the norm. Average citizens will be expected to look after themselves and solve some of their problems through their own initiative, self-respect and firm set of values.

After many years of emphasis on illness and disease, we now become educated toward maintaining good health by proper diet and exercise. The days of deliberately abusing the system with overdrinking, overeating or overmedication with the resultant whining and complaining for the doctors to miraculously make us well while the government pays the bill, are hopefully dwindling. We have learned the hard lesson that it is our own responsibility to take care of our own bodies, not the medical profession's, and not the government's.

All in all, this is an excellent transit to straighten out the obvious inequities in government laws and regulations, to structure it in a new concept which is clear cut, easy to understand and fair to all. All citizens should feel the results in being able to satisfy their daily needs and still have something left to stash away for Saturnian security.

Saturn in Aquarius Square Pluto in Scorpio

Square starts in March, 1992, with Saturn at 14 degrees of Aquarius and Pluto at 23 degrees of Scorpio: exact square in March, 1993, with Saturn at 24 degrees of Aquarius and Pluto at 25 degrees of Scorpio: exact square from October, 1993, to December, 1993, with Saturn at 23, 24, 25 degrees in Aquarius and Pluto at 23, 24, 25 degrees of Scorpio: square ends in January, 1994, with Saturn at 29 degrees of Aquarius and Pluto at 27 degrees of Scorpio.

In square aspect to Scorpio, the rigidity of Saturn may affect Aquarius uneasily. The Aquarian intellect may be so structured and controlled by the Saturn dominance that their free-form ideas and new world concepts never make it to the drawing board. The opposite result occurs when the Aquarian scientist creates innovative plans and startling inventions which are useable on a practical level for humankind.

On the other angle, Pluto in Scorpio struggles to infuse the Aquarian nature with more feeling and to instill intellectual achievements with consideration for their ultimate result.

This stress could manifest in several ways.

Saturn in Aquarius controls humanity, in a sense. But too much control exercised unwisely can cause havoc and ruin to a country and its citizens. Our urgency in today's world stems from the misuse of the earth's resources and what is happening to the balance of nature as a result. Are we polluting the oceans, the earth and the air with our over-production, our desperate need for energy? Are we exhausting the forests, our mineral supplies killing off the wild creatures to keep ourselves going in the manner to which we have become accustomed?

The conglomerates, which operate as kingdoms unto themselves, may tell us they are producing what the populace demands but on closer inspection we may discover they are destroying those vital resources we must have to survive in the future. Pluto in Scorpio lets loose its emotional power, its ability to go beneath the surface to investigate, to clean out the dark corners, to find out what is actually happening in our ever dwindling universe. We may be appalled as the final bill comes up for payment.

The Saturn control coupled with the Aquarian detachment can manifest in a loss of identity for ourselves as little by little the machines encroach on our lives. Are we to end up merely as a number programmed into a giant world-wide computer? This ever-present danger rises up in full force during this transit.

The inherent interest in brotherhood that Aquarius expresses must not be overwhelmed by the more rigid structure of Saturn exercising too much control. During this two-and-a-half year period, much tension will develop with the fixed square in operation. Let us hope that the influences of the planets and signs involved will find expression of their positive qualities in a rational way.

Saturn in Pisces Trine Pluto in Scorpio

The trine begins in May, 1995, with Saturn at 22 degrees of Pisces and Pluto at 29 degrees of Scorpio. It ends in November, 1995, with Saturn at 18 degrees of Pisces and Pluto at 29 degrees of Scorpio. It continues in fire-signs through April, 1997.

As the turbulent twentieth century nears its close, the emotions of Pisces and Scorpio find full, but controlled expression in the trine. The hand of authority in government and law now is touched with justice and mercy as it reaches out to the populace in a spirit of love and renewal. A beneficient world-wide government may have been successfully established. Careful use of energy, the land and air will by this time have been executed into laws protecting individuals and their rights to healthy surroundings. Pluto has investigated methods of using the limitless resources of the sea and the underground and found acceptable ways to employ their elements in harmony with the earth's environment.

It is generally believed that the Piscean Age draws to a close near the end of this century and the Aquarian Age begins. It is fitting that this time span we have known ends with Saturn, the planet of discipline, in Pisces, the sign of compassion and universal love. For now we can shut the door on materialism and open the door to a higher evolvement than man has ever aspired to before in the darkness of the ages that have led the way to this new beginning. Pisces in trine to Scorpio, brings us a view of where we came from and what we can transcend to as we give joyful welcome to the age of Aquarius.

Conclusion

An honest effort has been made to project the power of Pluto into the future. Although we can recognize the limitations of delineation without the individual's natal chart to reinforce or modify the basic factors, we leave the proof of truth to the generations of tomorrow. Hopefully, the reader will be guided by an objective and sincere desire to expand this groundwork.

It is extremely important to be aware of the fact that one's own thoughts on this matter can serve the future well. Ask those questions that defy logical explanation. Do not accept these words as infinite wisdom. Seek the truth in your own chart and, should you find the truth, test it carefully in the charts of your clients and friends.

Bibliography

1. Prete, J. Robert & Gallo, Angela, *Celebrity Horoscopes,* Rising Sign Publishing Company 1975.
2. Jansky, Robert Carl, *Astrology and the Feminist Movement,* Astro-Analytics 1977.
3. Jansky, Robert Carl, *Horoscopes Here and Now,* Astro-Analytics 1974.
4. *Circle Book of Charts,* Circle Books 1972.
5. "Mercury Hour" Magazine, Lynchburg, Virginia.
6. From the files of Lois M. Rodden.
7. American Federation of Astrologers, Tempe, Arizona.
8. "Horoscope Magazine," Dell Publishing Company, New York.
9. Data supplied by subject.
10. San Diego Astrological Society.
11. From the files of Marc Penfield.
12. Public Records.
13. From the files of Joan McEvers.
14. Arroyo, Stephen, *Astrology Karma and Transformation,* CRCS Publications, 1978.